KT-473-025

cupcakes

essential recipes

Publisher's Note:
Raw or semi-cooked eggs should not be consumed by babies, toddlers,
pregnant or breastfeeding women, the elderly or those suffering from a chronic illness.

Publisher & Creative Director: Nick Wells
Senior Project Editor: Catherine Taylor
Photography: Colin Bowling
Home economist and stylist: Ann Nicol
Copy Editor: Constance Novis
Art Director: Mike Spender
Layout Design: Jane Ashley
Digital Design & Production: Chris Herbert
Proofreader: Dawn Laker

Special thanks to Digby Smith and Helen Wall, and to the following for supplying materials for photography:

For all cake-decorating supplies by mail order, such as paper cases, sugarpaste, fondant, icing colours and equipment and bakeware:
Squires Group, Squires House, 3 Waverley Lane, Farnham, Surrey, GU9 8BB. Tel: 0845 22 55 67 1/2. www.squires-shop.com

For bakeware, muffin tins and trays and paper cases by mail order:
Lakeland, Alexandria Buildings, Windermere, Cumbria, LA23 1BQ. Tel: 01539 488 100. www.lakeland.co.uk

This is a Flame Tree book

FLAME TREE PUBLISHING
Crabtree Hall, Crabtree Lane
Fulham, London SW6 6TY
United Kingdom
www.flametreepublishing.com

Flame Tree is part of The Foundry Creative Media Company Limited

First published 2011

Copyright © 2011 Flame Tree Publishing

12 14 13 11
3 5 7 9 10 8 6 4 2

ISBN: 978-1-84786-967-8

All rights reserved. No part of this publication may be reproduced, stored in a retrieval system, or transmitted in any form or by any means,
electronic, mechanical, photocopying, recording or otherwise, without the prior written permission of the publisher.

A copy of the CIP data for this book is available from the British Library.

Printed in China

cupcakes

essential recipes

Ann Nicol

FLAME TREE
PUBLISHING

Contents

Celebrate & Party 110

Seasonal Fun 184

Introduction

Why are cupcakes and muffins so popular? They seem to be on sale everywhere these days, but, as these little cakes are so quick and easy (you will find that most of the recipes in this book take under half an hour to bake), it is so simple to make your own. Cupcakes, fairy cakes and muffins are delightful and versatile – ideal for breakfast, an informal tea, a special occasion or for children's parties.

There is no comparison to the quality of home-made cakes and the fun to be had in making and baking them, and, as shop-bought cakes are expensive, you will notice the difference in price too. You also have plenty of scope for decorating, so you can create tailor-made treats for all sorts of occasions.

As a gift or a centrepiece, a batch of cupcakes or muffins brings a personal touch to any celebration, from a wedding anniversary to a children's party. This book has cakes for every occasion, some very quick and easy, some requiring a little more patience. If you are short on time, I have included tips on preparing ahead and freezing to make life easy.

Baking is a good way to introduce children to the art of cookery and these recipes will help to teach the basic techniques. Children also love the decorating part, and there are lots of ideas here to choose from.

So what is the best part of baking cupcakes and muffins? Well, they give so much pleasure: you get a real sense of satisfaction when you create a fresh batch of delicious bakes, accompanied by the marvellous aroma of baking that fills your home; and just watch the delighted reaction when you give them to your friends and neighbours.

How to Use This Book

This book is aimed at both those new to baking and experienced bakers, and shows how to create these popular mini-cakes, from the right equipment and ingredients to the cake and its decoration.

Just follow our simple step-by-step guides to ensure successful results. The choice is yours – you can make deep muffins, the shallower cupcakes and delicate fairy cakes, or mini muffins. The size of each cake will depend on the depth of your tins and how deeply you fill the paper cases.

This book is divided into sections that deal with different types of cakes, including family favourites and fairy cakes for teatime treats, luscious chocolate cakes, and small cakes decorated for special occasions such as birthdays, Mother's Day, weddings and Christmas.

Baking and cake decoration involves many different techniques and a little skill is needed for certain cakes, but you will build up your confidence through practice.

To help you achieve success every time, there are tips on choosing the right type of muffin and bun tins and paper liners. Using the very best ingredients is important, as are utensils and careful weighing and measuring. You will not achieve good results without first checking your oven for correct temperatures and exact timings (*see* below).

Check Your Oven

Each recipe begins with an oven setting, and it is important to preheat the oven to the correct temperature before placing the cakes in to bake. As well as preheating the oven, it is important to arrange the shelves in the correct position in the oven before you start. The best baking position for cupcakes is just above the centre of the oven and best results are achieved by baking only one tray at a time. If you bake two trays at once, you may find the lower tray will come out with flatter tops to the cakes.

Many of us have fan-assisted ovens. These circulate hot air round the oven and heat up very quickly. For fan ovens, you will need to reduce the temperature stated in the recipe by 10 per cent, which is usually 20˚C. For example, if the stated temperature in a recipe is 180˚C, reduce it to 160˚C for a fan-assisted oven. However, ovens do vary, so follow your manufacturer's instructions and get to know the way your oven heats. If your oven is too hot, the outsides of the cakes will

burn before the interior has had time to cook. If it is too cool, the cakes may sink or not rise evenly. Try not to open the oven door until at least halfway through the baking time, when the cakes have had time to rise and set, as a sudden drop in temperature will stop the cakes rising and they may sink.

Weighing and Measuring

All of the recipes in this book give metric and imperial measurements, but you must stick to one set only – i.e. only ever use either metric or imperial in one recipe, as they are not exact equivalents.

All spoon measurements should be used level (as opposed to 'heaped') for accuracy, and always use a recognised set of metric or imperial spoon measures for best results. Do not use domestic teaspoons and tablespoons as measures, as these may be deeper or shallower than a proper measuring spoon. Never estimate weights, as you will not achieve an accurate result.

Ingredients for baking should be weighed exactly and good kitchen scales are a vital piece of equipment for a baker. Old-fashioned scales with a pan and a set of weights or modern ones with a digital display screen are equally good, as long as they are accurate. A measuring jug is vital for liquids and it needs to be marked with small measures for smaller amounts.

Essential Equipment

Trays and Cases

Metal Muffin Trays

Muffin trays come in different weights and sizes. The standard-size muffin tray has 12 holes, about 3 cm/1¼ inches deep, but they are also available with six deeper-set holes or with shallower indentations of about 2 cm/⁷⁄₈ inch depth (often known as 'bun trays' or 'fairy-cake trays'), for making smaller cupcakes, or even with 'mini' size holes (see below).

When purchasing, buy the heaviest tray you can afford – although these will be expensive, they produce the best results because they distribute the heat well and do not buckle. If using trays without a nonstick finish, it is advisable to give these a light greasing before use. To grease trays, apply a thin film of melted vegetable margarine with a pastry brush or rub round the tin with kitchen paper and a little softened butter or margarine. You will normally need to line metal muffin trays with deep paper muffin cases or strips of baking parchment.

Mini-muffin Trays

These have small individual holes that can be half the diameter of holes in the bigger muffin trays, and as shallow as 1.75 cm/¾ inch deep (see page 220). They can be made of metal, but the silicone pans are particularly useful for mini muffins because they turn out so easily and give a good shape.

Silicone Muffin Trays and Cupcake Cases

These are flexible and produce very good results. Although they are sold as nonstick, it is still advisable to rub round each hole or case with a little oil on kitchen paper to prevent sticking. Silicone cupcake cases come in many bright colours and, unlike paper

cases, are reusable. Simply wash out any crumbs after use in soapy water and leave them to dry, or clean them in the dishwasher.

Paper Cases

These come in many varieties, colours and shapes. It is advisable to buy the more expensive types, which are thicker and give a good shape to the cake as it rises. Oil and moisture is less likely to penetrate through the thicker cases, whereas it may show through the cheaper ones. Metallic gold, silver and coloured cupcake cases give good results and create a stunning effect for a special occasion. Cupcake cases also come in mini-muffin sizes. These may not be so easy to find, but can be bought from mail-order cake decoration suppliers.

Baking Papers and Foil

Nonstick baking 'parchment' or 'paper' is useful for lining the bases of small tins or for drying out chocolate and sugarpaste shapes, while greaseproof paper is needed for making triangular paper icing bags. Baking parchment can be used, but greaseproof paper is better, as it is thinner and more flexible. A large sheet of kitchen foil is handy for wrapping cakes or for protecting wrapped cakes in the freezer.

Electric Mixers

A hand-held electric mixer makes quick work of whisking butter and sugar and is an invaluable aid for cake-baking, while a large tabletop mixer is useful if you are making larger quantities of muffins and is good for whisking frostings and buttercream in larger quantities. Do not be tempted to use a food processor for mixing small amounts, as it is easy to over-process and this may produce flat cakes.

Other Essential Items

In addition to the usual variety of mixing bowls, wooden spoons, measuring spoons, scissors, sieves, graters, skewers for testing cakes and wire racks for cooling, the following are particularly useful in cupcake-making.

Pastry Brush

A pastry brush is used for brushing glazes over cakes and melted butter round tins. As brushes tend to wear out regularly and shed their bristles, keep a spare new brush to hand.

Palette Knives

A small and a large palette knife are ideal for many jobs, including loosening cakes from their tins, lifting cakes and swirling on buttercream icing. A palette knife with a cranked blade is useful for lifting small cakes or flat pieces of sugarpaste.

Stamps and Cutters

Stamps and cutters for almost any imaginable shape can be bought from specialist cake and baking stores. They come in classic metal cookie-cutter styles, in plastic, or as plunger-style. If you do not have appropriate cutters, you can use images found in books or magazines as templates.

Piping Bags and Nozzles

A nylon piping bag that comes with a set of five nozzles is a very useful piece of equipment for decorating with icings. Look for a set with a plain nozzle and various star nozzles for piping swirls round cupcakes. The larger the star nozzle, the wider the swirls will be on the finished cake. Disposable paper or clear plastic icing bags are available, but nylon piping bags can be washed in warm soapy water and dried out, ready to re-use again and again.

To Make a Paper Icing Bag

Cut out a 38 x 25.5 cm/15 x 10 inch rectangle of greaseproof paper. Fold it diagonally in half to form two triangular shapes. Cut along the fold line to make two triangles. One of these triangles can be used another time – it is quicker and easier to make two at a time from one square than to measure and mark out a triangle on a sheet of paper.

Fold one of the points on the long side of the triangle over the top to make a sharp cone and hold in the centre. Fold the other sharp end of the triangle over the cone. Hold all the points together at the back of the cone, keeping the pointed end sharp. Turn the points inside the top edge, fold over to make a crease, then secure with a piece of sticky tape. To use, snip away the end, place a piping nozzle in position and fill the bag with icing, or fill the bag with icing first, then snip away a tiny hole at the end for piping a plain edge, writing or piping tiny dots.

Ingredients

In cupcake-making, the classic cake base is made in the same way as any typical cake – that is, by mixing sugar, fats, flour and eggs together and varying with further ingredients or different methods to achieve the required result. This is a *selected* outline of ingredients more relevant to cupcake-making.

'Softened' Butter

Remember that if a recipe calls for 'softened' butter (or hard-block margarine) it means you should remove it from the refrigerator before using – it is easier to mix in when at room temperature.

Yogurt and Buttermilk

Plain yogurt is great for adding richness and moisture to smaller cakes. Do not use low-fat yogurt – stick to plain, thick natural yogurts that have more substance to them.

Buttermilk is produced by adding bacteria to low-fat milk to thicken and sour it. This is used in recipes for small cakes and muffins that use bicarbonate of soda, as the acidity from the buttermilk produces carbon dioxide, which raises the cakes. Buttermilk will give an extra lift to cupcakes. You will find buttermilk on sale in the dairy section of larger supermarkets but, if it is not available, use 1 tbsp lemon juice to 300 ml/10 fl oz plain yogurt or whole milk as a substitute.

Flavourings

Flavouring extracts are very concentrated and usually sold in liquid form in small bottles. A teaspoon measure will usually be enough to flavour a mixture for 12 cakes. Vanilla and almond extracts are ideal to impart their delicate flavours into cake mixtures and you will find the more expensive extracts give a finer and more natural flavour. Rosewater can be used for flavouring

both cake mixtures and icings and has a delicate, perfumed flavour. Fruit flavourings, such as lemon, lime, orange and raspberry, will give a fresh twist.

Chocolate

For the best results and a professional finish and flavour, it is always advisable to buy the highest quality chocolate you can find, although this will be more expensive. Better-quality chocolates contain a higher percentage of real cocoa fat, which gives a flavour and texture far superior to cheaper varieties. (Cheaper chocolate labelled as 'cooking' or 'baking' chocolate contains a much smaller percentage of cocoa solids and is best avoided in favour of better-quality eating chocolate.) The amount of cocoa fat or solids contained in chocolate will be marked on the wrapper of any good-quality chocolate. Those marked as having 70 percent cocoa solids will give the best results and you will find this chocolate is shiny and brittle and it should snap very easily.

Dark Chocolate

Also known as 'plain' or 'plain dark' chocolate, this is the most useful all-purpose type of chocolate for baking, as it has a good strong flavour.

Milk Chocolate

Milk chocolate has sugar added and is sweeter than dark, so is good for melting for icings and decorations.

White Chocolate

This is not strictly chocolate, as it contains only cocoa butter, milk and sugar. It is expensive and the most difficult to work with, so must be used with care. It is best to grate it finely and keep the temperature very low when melting it.

Chocolate Cake Covering

This is a cheaper substitute containing a minimum of 2.5 percent cocoa solids and vegetable oil. It is considerably cheaper than real chocolate and the flavour is not so good, but it is easy to melt and sets quickly and well for a coating.

Chocolate Chips

Chips come in dark, milk and white varieties and are sold in small bags. They are useful for adding to cupcake and muffin mixtures to enrich them and add a delicious texture as they part melt into the cakes on baking.

Cocoa Powder

Cocoa powder needs to be cooked to release the full flavour, so blend it with boiling water to make into a paste, then cool, before adding to a recipe, or sift it into the bowl with the flour.

Drinking Chocolate

Be aware that this is not the same as cocoa powder, as it contains milk powder and sugar. Some recipes may specify using drinking chocolate and these are successful, but do not substitute it for cocoa powder, as it will spoil the flavour of a cake.

For Decorating

Icing Sugar

Icing sugar is fine and powdery. It is usually sold plain and white, but can also be bought as an unrefined golden (or 'natural') variety. Use it for delicate icings, frostings and decorations. Store this sugar in a dry place, as it can absorb moisture and this will make it go hard and lumpy. Always sift this sugar at least once, or preferably twice, before you use it, to remove any hard lumps that would prevent icing from achieving a smooth texture – lumpy icing is impossible to pipe out.

Fondant Icing Sugar

This is sold in plain and flavoured varieties and gives a beautiful glossy finish to cake toppings. Just add a little boiled water to the sugar, according to the packet instructions, to make a shiny icing that can be poured or drizzled over cupcake tops to give a very professional finish. Colour the plain white icing with a few spots of paste food colouring to achieve your desired result.

Flavoured fondant icing sugar is sold in strawberry, raspberry, orange, lemon and blackcurrant flavours and also has colouring added. These sugars are ideal if you want to make a large batch of cakes with different coloured and flavoured toppings. Flavoured fondant sugars can also be whisked with softened unsalted butter and cream cheese to make delicious frostings in just a few moments.

Royal Icing Sugar

Royal icing sets to a classic, firm Christmas-cake-style covering. Sold in packs as plain white sugar, this is whisked with cold water to give an instant royal icing. It has dried egg white included in the mixture, so does not need the long beating that traditional royal icing recipes require. It is also ideal to use for those who cannot eat raw egg whites.

Tubes of Writing Icing

You can buy small tubes of ready-coloured royal icing or gel icing, usually in sets of black, red, yellow and blue, and these are ideal for small amounts of writing or for piping on dots or small decorations.

Food Colourings

You can buy food colourings in liquid, paste, gel and powder or dust forms in a great range of colours.

Paste food colourings These are best for using with sugarpaste. They are sold in small tubs and are very concentrated, so should be added to the sugarpaste dot by dot on the end of a wooden cocktail stick. Knead the colouring in evenly, adding more until you get the colour you require.

Liquid and gel food colourings Gel colourings are ideal for adding to frostings. Add this cautiously drop by drop, beating the frosting well until you reach the colour you require.

Dusts and sparkle colourings These should be lightly brushed onto dry sugarpaste to form a delicate sheen to decorations such as flowers.

Bought Sugar Decorations and Sprinkles

A selection of pretty sprinkles can be bought in supermarkets or by mail order from specialist cake decorating companies, and these provide a wonderful way to make quick and easy cake toppings.

Basic Techniques

Different Making Methods

Creaming

Light cakes are made by the creaming method, which means that the butter and sugar are first beaten or 'creamed' together. A little care is needed for this method. Use a large mixing bowl to beat the fat and sugar together until pale and fluffy. The eggs are gradually beaten in to form a slackened batter and the flour is folded in last, to stiffen up the mixture.

Rubbing In

In this method, the fat is lightly worked into the flour between the fingers, as in pastry-making, until the mixture resembles fine crumbs. This can be done by hand or in a food processor. Enough liquid is stirred in to give a soft mixture that will drop easily from a spoon. This method is used for easy fruit cakes and small buns such as rock cakes.

All-In-One Mixtures

This 'one stage' method is quick and easy and is perfect for those new to baking, as it does not involve any complicated techniques. It is ideal for making light sponges, but soft tub-type margarine or softened butter (i.e. at room temperature) must be used. All the ingredients are simply placed in a large bowl and quickly beaten together for just a few minutes until smooth. Be careful not to over-beat, as this will make the mixture too wet. Self-raising flour with the addition of a little extra baking powder is vital for a good rise.

The Melting Method

Cakes with a delicious moist, sticky texture, such as gingerbread, are made by this method. These cakes use a high proportion of sugar and syrup, which are gently warmed together in a saucepan with the fat, until the sugar has dissolved and the mixture is liquid. It is important to cool the hot melted mixture a little before beating in flour, eggs and spices to make a batter, otherwise it will damage the power of the raising agent.

Checking to See if the Cakes Are Cooked

Small cupcakes and muffins should be golden, risen and firm to the touch when pressed lightly in the centre. The last part of a cupcake or muffin to cook is the centre, so, after the baking time stated, check this area. For light sponge-type cakes, press the centre lightly with the fingertips and, if the cake is cooked, it should spring back easily. To test more thoroughly, insert a thin warmed skewer into the deepest part of the centre. If the cake is cooked, it will come out perfectly clean, with no mixture sticking to it, but, if there is some on the skewer, bake the cakes for a little longer and test again.

Cooling the Cakes

All freshly baked cakes are very fragile; they need time to stand in the tins to cool for a short time to make them firm. Sponges and delicate cupcakes need standing time of about 2 minutes, muffins need 3–4 minutes and fruity mixtures need 5 minutes.

If muffins start to stick to their moulds, leave until the cakes are firm, then loosen their sides by running round the tins with a small palette knife. Carefully turn the cakes out on a wire rack to cool. Do not leave cupcakes in paper cases in the bun trays to cool completely, as moisture that collects in the bun trays will cause the paper cases to go damp and discolour.

How to Patch Up Mistakes

- If your cakes have peaked, then these can easily be trimmed flat when the cakes are cold (see below).

- If the cakes have overcooked or are burnt on the outside, simply scrape this away with a serrated knife and cover the surface with buttercream.

- If the cakes are a little dry, sprinkle them with a few drops of sweet sherry or orange juice.

Cutting the Tops Level

Many cupcakes will form a small peak while baking and this is an ideal shape for coating with buttercream or piping round a swirl of cream cheese icing. However, some methods of decorating cakes require a flat surface, so, for these, trim the tops level with a sharp knife. Coat the cakes with apricot glaze and press on a disc of almond paste or sugarpaste to give you a flat surface to decorate.

Storing Cupcakes and Muffins

- Make sure cakes are completely cold before storing, otherwise condensation can form in the container and this can cause the cakes to go mouldy.

- Large, flat plastic food containers are ideal for cupcakes and muffins, as they enable the cakes to be kept flat in one single layer and will keep small cakes moist. Old-fashioned cake tins can be used, but they do not hold a large number of small cakes. If you do not have a large cake container, invert a large mixing bowl over the cakes on a plate or flat surface and the cakes will stay fresh.

- Sponge cakes will keep for 3–4 days, and richer fruit cakes for 5 days to a week. Cakes with fresh cream fillings and decorations need to be kept in the refrigerator and are best eaten on the day of filling with cream.

- Store cakes with sugarpaste decorations in a cool place, but not in the refrigerator. The moisture in a refrigerator will be absorbed by the sugarpaste and make this icing go limp and soggy.

Freezing Cupcakes

Most cupcakes will freeze well but, for best results, freeze undecorated. Completely cool each cake and freeze in one layer on a baking sheet or flat tray. Once frozen, place in strong freezer bags or boxes and seal to exclude as much air as possible, label and freeze. Cakes containing fresh fruits such as blueberries or raspberries will not freeze well, as the fruit tends to make the cakes soggy when thawed, so these are best eaten fresh on the day of baking. To use frozen cakes, completely unwrap and thaw at room temperature on racks. The paper cases may peel away from frozen cakes, so these may need to be replaced with fresh ones before decorating the cakes.

Basic Cake Recipes

Basic Vanilla Cupcakes

Makes 18 deep cupcakes, 24 fairy cakes or 36 mini muffins

225 g/8 oz butter, softened
225 g/8 oz caster sugar
4 medium eggs, beaten
225 g/8 oz self-raising flour
$1/2$ tsp baking powder
2 tbsp semi-skimmed milk
1 tsp vanilla extract
1 tsp glycerine

Preheat the oven to 180°C/350°F/Gas Mark 4 and line appropriate trays with enough paper cases. Whisk the butter and sugar together, preferably with an electric hand mixer, until pale and fluffy. Whisk in the egg gradually, adding a teaspoon of flour with each addition to prevent the mixture from curdling.

Sift the remaining flour and baking powder into the bowl, then gradually whisk in the milk, extract and glycerine. Spoon the mixture into the paper cases and bake for 25 minutes for the larger cakes, 15 minutes for the fairy cakes or 12 minutes for the mini muffins, or until firm and golden. Cool on a wire rack. Keep for 3–4 days in an airtight container.

Mini Cupcakes

Makes about 24

100 g/$3^1/2$ oz golden caster sugar
100 g/$3^1/2$ oz butter, softened
finely grated zest and juice of $1/2$ lemon
2 medium eggs, beaten
100 g/$3^1/2$ oz self-raising flour
2 tsp milk

Preheat the oven to 190°C/375°F/Gas Mark 5. Grease a mini-muffin tray or line it with mini paper cases. Put the sugar, butter and lemon zest in a large bowl and beat until light and fluffy. Add the beaten egg a little at a time, with a teaspoon of flour with each addition. Fold in the flour, lemon juice and milk and mix until smooth.

Spoon into the mini-muffin tray or cases and bake for about 12 minutes until golden and risen. Transfer to a rack to cool. Keep for 2–3 days in an airtight container.

Individual Fruit Cakes

Makes 18 fairy cakes

125 g/4 oz butter
125 g/4 oz soft dark muscovado sugar
2 medium eggs, beaten
225 g/8 oz self-raising flour
1 tsp ground mixed spice
finely grated zest, and 1 tbsp juice,
    of 1 orange
1 tbsp black treacle
350 g/12 oz mixed dried fruit

Preheat the oven to 180°C/350°F/Gas Mark 4. Line a fairy-cake muffin tray with paper cases. Beat the butter and sugar together until light and fluffy, then beat in the eggs a little at a time, adding a teaspoon of flour with each addition. Sift in the remaining flour and spice, add the orange zest and juice, treacle and dried fruit to the bowl and fold together until the mixture is blended.

Spoon into the tins and bake for 30 minutes until firm in the centre and a skewer comes out clean. Leave to cool in the tins for 15 minutes, then turn out to cool on a wire rack. Store in an airtight container for up to 4 weeks or freeze until needed.

Quick All-in-One Mix for Cupcakes

Makes 12 deep cupcakes or 18 fairy cakes

125 g/4 oz caster sugar
125 g/4 oz soft-tub margarine
2 medium eggs
125 g/4 oz self-raising flour
1 tsp milk or lemon juice

Preheat the oven to 190°C/375°F/Gas Mark 5. Line appropriate trays with enough paper cases for the cakes. Place all the cake ingredients in a large bowl and beat with an electric mixer for about 2 minutes until smooth. Half-fill the paper cases with the mixture. Bake for about 15 minutes until firm, risen and golden. Remove to a wire rack to cool. Keep for 2–3 days in an airtight container.

Carrot Cupcakes

**Makes 12 deep cupcakes, 18 cupcakes or
22 mini cupcakes**

225 g/8 oz carrots, peeled
175 g/6 oz self-raising wholemeal flour
1 tsp baking powder
$^1/_2$ tsp ground cinnamon
pinch salt
150 ml/$^1/_4$ pt sunflower oil
150 g/5 oz soft light brown sugar
3 medium eggs, beaten
1 tsp vanilla extract
50 g/2 oz sultanas or raisins

Chocolate Fudge Cakes

**Makes 12 deep cupcakes, 18 cupcakes or
22 mini cupcakes**

150 g/5 oz butter, softened
150 g/5 oz golden caster sugar
3 medium eggs, beaten
125 g/4 oz self-raising flour
25 g/1 oz cocoa powder
1 tbsp milk

Preheat the oven to 190˚C/375˚F/Gas Mark 5. Line appropriate trays with enough foil or paper cake cases. Place the butter, caster sugar and eggs in a large bowl and then sift in the flour and cocoa powder. Whisk together with the milk for about 2 minutes until smooth, then spoon into the cases, filling them two-thirds full.

Bake for about 20 minutes for the deep cakes, 14 minutes for the cupcakes or 12–14 minutes for the mini cupcakes until well risen and springy to the touch. Cool on a wire rack. Keep for 3 days in an airtight container.

Preheat the oven to 180˚C/350˚F/Gas Mark 4. Lightly oil or line appropriate trays with enough paper cases for the cakes. Grate the carrots finely. Sift the flour, baking powder, cinnamon and salt into a bowl, then tip in any bran from the sieve. Add the oil, sugar, eggs, extract, sultanas and grated carrots.

Beat until smooth, then spoon into the muffin trays. Bake for 25 minutes for the deep cakes, 20 minutes for the cupcakes or 15–20 minutes for the mini muffins until risen and golden. Cool on a wire rack. Keep for 5 days in an airtight container.

Basic Icing Recipes

Cream Cheese Frosting

Covers 12 small cakes

50 g/2 oz unsalted butter, softened
300 g/11 oz icing sugar, sifted
flavouring of choice
food colourings of choice
125 g/4 oz full-fat cream cheese

Beat the butter and icing sugar together until light and fluffy. Add flavourings and colourings of choice and beat again. Add the cream cheese and whisk until light and fluffy. Do not over-beat, however, as the mixture can become runny.

Basic Buttercream Frosting

Covers 12 small cakes

150 g/5 oz unsalted butter, softened
225 g/8 oz icing sugar, sifted
2 tbsp hot milk or water

1 tsp vanilla extract
food colourings of choice

Beat the butter until light and fluffy, then beat in the sifted icing sugar and hot milk or water in two batches. Add the vanilla extract and any food colourings. Store chilled for up to two days in a lidded container.

Royal Icing

Makes 500 g/1 !b 2 oz to cover 12 deep muffins

2 medium egg whites
500 g/1 lb 2 oz icing sugar, sifted
2 tsp lemon juice

Put the egg whites in a large bowl and whisk lightly with a fork to break up the whites until foamy. Sift in half the icing sugar with the lemon juice and beat well with an electric mixer for 4 minutes or by hand with a wooden spoon for about 10 minutes until smooth.

Gradually sift in the remaining icing sugar and beat again until thick, smooth and brilliant white and the icing forms soft peaks when flicked up with a spoon. Keep the royal icing covered with a clean damp cloth until you are ready to use it, or store in the refrigerator in a tightly lidded plastic container until needed. If making royal icing ahead of time to use later, beat it again before use to remove any air bubbles that may have formed in the mixture.

Tip For a softer royal icing that will not set too hard, beat 1 tsp glycerine into the mixture.

Glacé Icing

Covers 12 small cakes

225 g/8 oz icing sugar
few drops lemon juice or vanilla or almond extract
2–3 tbsp boiling water
liquid food colouring (optional)

Sift the icing sugar into a bowl and add the chosen flavouring. Gradually stir in enough water to mix to a consistency of thick cream. Beat with a wooden spoon until the icing is thick enough to coat the back of the spoon. Add colouring, if liked, and use at once, as the icing will begin to form a skin.

Apricot Glaze

Makes 450 g/1 lb to cover 24 small cakes

450 g/1 lb apricot jam
3 tbsp water
1 tsp lemon juice

Place the jam, water and juice in a heavy-based saucepan and heat gently, stirring, until soft and melted. Boil rapidly for 1 minute, then press through a fine sieve with the back of a wooden spoon. Discard the pieces of fruit. Use immediately for glazing or sticking on almond paste, or pour into a clean jar or plastic lidded container and store in the refrigerator for up to 3 months.

Almond Paste

Makes 450 g/1 lb to cover 24 small cakes

125 g/4 oz sifted icing sugar
125 g/4 oz caster sugar
225 g/8 oz ground almonds
1 medium egg
1 tsp lemon juice

Stir the sugars and ground almonds together in a bowl. Whisk the egg and lemon juice together and mix into the dry ingredients. Knead until the paste is smooth. Wrap tightly in clingfilm or foil to keep airtight and store in the refrigerator until needed. The paste can be made 2–3 days ahead of time, but, after that, it will start to dry out and become difficult to handle.

To use the almond paste, knead on a surface lightly dusted with icing sugar until soft and pliable. Brush the top of each cake with apricot glaze. Roll out the almond paste and cut out discs large enough to cover the tops of the cakes. Press onto the cakes.

Sugarpaste Icing

Makes 350 g/12 oz to cover 12 small cakes or use for decorations

1 medium egg white
1 tbsp liquid glucose
350 g/12 oz icing sugar, sifted

Place the egg white and liquid glucose in a large mixing bowl and stir together with a fork, breaking up the egg white. Add the icing sugar gradually, mixing in with a

palette knife until the mixture binds together and forms a ball. Turn the ball of icing out onto a clean surface dusted with icing sugar and knead for 5 minutes until soft but firm enough to roll out. If the icing is too soft, knead in a little more icing sugar until the mixture is pliable.

To colour, knead in paste food colouring. Do not use liquid food colouring, as this is not suitable and will make the sugarpaste go limp.

To use, roll out thinly on a clean surface dusted with icing sugar and cut out discs large enough to cover the top of each cake. Brush the almond paste (if using as a layer underneath the sugarpaste discs) with a little cold boiled water or a clear spirit such as kirsch and press onto the cake, then press the sugarpaste on top of the almond paste topping. Alternatively, coat the cakes with a little buttercream, place the sugarpaste disc on top and press down.

To shape, knead lightly and roll out thinly on a surface dusted with icing sugar. Use cutters or templates to make flowers or shapes, or mould into shapes with your fingertips and leave to dry out for 24 hours in egg boxes lined with clingfilm.

Decorating

The microwave oven is ideal for melting chocolate. Place the chocolate pieces in a small microwave-proof bowl and melt gently on low or defrost settings in small bursts of 30 seconds, checking and stirring in between, until the chocolate has melted.

Making Chocolate Decorations

Curls and shavings Spread melted chocolate out thinly onto a clean dry surface such as a plastic board, marble or a clean worktop. Leave the chocolate until almost set, then pull a long sharp-bladed knife through it at an angle to form curls or shavings. Place the curls in a lidded plastic box in the refrigerator until needed for decoration.

Using Chocolate

Melting Chocolate

Care and attention is needed to melt chocolate for baking and cake decorating needs. If the chocolate gets too hot or comes into contact with water or steam, it will 'seize' or stiffen and form into a hard ball instead of a smooth melted mixture. You can add a little vegetable oil or margarine, a teaspoon at a time, to the mixture to make it liquid again.

To melt chocolate, break the bar into small pieces, or grate or chop it, and place in a heatproof bowl standing over a bowl of warm, not hot, water. Make sure the bowl containing the chocolate is completely dry and that steam or water cannot enter the bowl. Heat the water to a gentle simmer only and leave the bowl to stand for about 5 minutes. Do not let the water get too hot or the chocolate will reach too high a temperature and will lose its sheen.

Leaves Wash and dry holly or rose leaves and place on a sheet of nonstick baking parchment. Melt the chocolate and paint on the underside of each leaf. Leave to dry out, then carefully peel away the leaf. You

Beat 1 medium egg white with 2 tsp cold water until frothy. Paint a thin layer of egg white carefully over the items, then sprinkle lightly with caster sugar, shaking to remove any excess. Leave to dry on a wire rack lined with nonstick baking parchment.

Using Buttercream and Cream Cheese Frostings

These soft icings can be swirled onto the tops of cupcakes with a small palette knife or placed in a piping bag fitted with a star nozzle to pipe impressive whirls.

will find the veined side is uppermost on the chocolate leaf. Place in a lidded container and keep refrigerated until needed for decoration.

Crystallising Petals, Flowers, Leaves and Berries

Wash and dry herbs and leaves such as rosemary sprigs and small bay leaves or berries such as cranberries. Separate edible petals from small flowers such as rosebuds and clean small flowers such as violets with a clean brush, but do not wash them.

- Do not be mean with the amount of frosting you use. If this is scraped on thinly, you will see the cake underneath, so be generous.

- Keep cupcakes with frostings in a cool place, or refrigerate, as they contain a high percentage of butter, which will melt easily in too warm a place.

- Cakes coated in buttercream can be decorated easily with colourful sprinkles and sugars. To make this easy, place the sprinkles in a small saucer or on a piece of nonstick baking parchment and roll the outside edges of each cake in the decorations.

Using Sugarpaste

Sugarpaste is a versatile icing, as it can be used for covering small cakes or modelling all sorts of fancy decorations. To use as a covering, roll out the sugarpaste thinly on a surface dusted with icing sugar and cut out circles the size of the cake tops. Coat each cake with a little apricot glaze or buttercream and press on the circles to form a flat surface.

Making Flat Decorations

To make letters, numbers or flat decorations, roll out the sugarpaste thinly and cut out the shapes free-hand or with cutters. You may have some templates or images that you would like to replicate, in which case trace the pattern you want onto a sheet of clear greaseproof paper or nonstick baking parchment, then position the paper over the sugarpaste. Mark over the pattern with the tip of a small sharp knife or a pin. Remove the paper and cut out the marked-on pattern with a small sharp knife. Leave your shapes to dry on nonstick baking parchment on a flat surface or a tray for 2–3 hours to make them firm and easy to handle.

Decorating Tips

• Always roll out almond paste or sugarpaste icing on a surface lightly dusted with icing sugar.

• Leave sugarpaste-covered cakes to firm up for 2 hours before adding decorations, as this provides a good finished surface to work on.

• Tie ribbons round the finished cake and secure them with a dab of royal icing. Never use pins in ribbons on a cake.

• Once decorated, store sugarpaste-covered cakes in large boxes in a cool place. Do not store in a refrigerator, as the sugarpaste will become damp and colours may run.

• Paste food colourings are best for working with sugarpaste and a little goes a very long way. As these are very concentrated, use a cocktail stick to add dots of paste gradually, until you are sure of the colour, and knead in until even.

Delicious & Dainty

Sometimes, there is nothing better than dainty sandwiches and pretty cakes, washed down with lashings of tea. This section includes classic cakes in cupcake form – from the unrivalled Lemon Drizzle to Coffee & Walnut. Delightful aromatic and flavoursome creations include Crystallised Violet and Lemon & Cardamom cupcakes. You will be spoilt for choice for your afternoon tea!

Lemon Drizzle Cupcakes

1 Preheat the oven to 180°C/350°F/Gas Mark 4 and line a 12-hole muffin tray with paper cases, or two bun trays with 18 fairy-cake paper cases.

2 Place the butter, sugar and eggs in a bowl and then sift in the flour and baking powder. Finely grate the zest of the lemon into the bowl.

3 Beat together for about 2 minutes, preferably with an electric hand mixer, until pale and fluffy. Spoon into the paper cases and bake for 25 minutes for the larger cupcakes or 15 minutes for the fairy cakes until firm and golden. Cool on a wire rack.

4 To make the topping, cut the zest from the other lemon into thin strips and set aside.

5 Squeeze the juice from the lemon into a small saucepan. Add the sugar and heat gently until every grain of sugar has dissolved. Add the strips of zest and cool slightly. Spoon the syrup and lemon strips over the cupcakes while still warm. Leave to cool. Keep for up to 4 days in an airtight container.

Ingredients

MAKES 12 DEEP CUPCAKES
OR 18 FAIRY CAKES

150 g/5 oz butter, softened
150 g/5 oz caster sugar
3 medium eggs, beaten
150 g/5 oz self-raising flour
½ tsp baking powder
1 lemon

To decorate:
1 lemon
50 g/2 oz caster sugar

Mini Carrot Cupcakes

1   Preheat the oven to 180°C/350°F/Gas Mark 4. Lightly oil two 12-hole mini-muffin trays. Grate the carrots.

2   Sift the flour, baking powder, cinnamon and salt into a bowl, with any bran from the sieve.

3   Add the oil, sugar, eggs, vanilla extract, sultanas and grated carrots. Beat until smooth, then spoon into the muffin trays. Bake for about 20 minutes until risen and golden. Cool on a wire rack.

4   To decorate, peel thin strips of zest from the orange. Beat the cream cheese and icing sugar together with 2 tsp juice from the orange to make a spreading consistency. Swirl the icing over each cupcake and then top with shreds of orange zest. Keep for up to 3 days in an airtight container in a cool place.

Ingredients
MAKES 22

175 g/6 oz self-raising
   wholemeal flour
1 tsp baking powder
$^1/_2$ tsp ground cinnamon
pinch salt
150 ml/$^1/_4$ pint sunflower oil
150 g/5 oz soft light brown sugar
3 medium eggs, beaten
1 tsp vanilla extract
50 g/2 oz sultanas
225 g/8 oz carrots, peeled

To decorate:
1 orange
75 g/3 oz cream cheese
175 g/6 oz golden icing sugar

1

3

3

Sticky Toffee Cupcakes

1 Preheat the oven to 180 C/350 F/Gas Mark 4. Line one or two bun trays with 16–18 fairy-cake cases, depending on the depth of the tray holes. Chop the dates, then place in a bowl with the bicarbonate of soda and pour over the hot water. Stir, then set aside to cool.

2 Sift the flour and baking powder into a bowl and add the diced butter. Rub in between your fingertips until the mixture resembles fine crumbs. Stir in the sugar and mix well. Add the egg, vanilla extract and the date mixture. Beat with a wooden spoon until smooth.

3 Spoon into the cases and bake for about 25 minutes until well risen and firm to the touch in the centre. Leave to cool in the tins for 5 minutes, then turn out to cool on a wire rack.

4 To make the topping, place the butter, sugar and cream in a small pan over a low heat and stir until the sugar dissolves. Bring to the boil and boil for 1–2 minutes until the mixture thickens. Brush quickly over each fairy cake, as the mixture will set as it cools. Keep for up to 2 days in an airtight container.

Ingredients

MAKES 16–18

50 g/5 oz stoned dates
1 tsp bicarbonate of soda
250 ml/8 fl oz hot water
175 g/6 oz plain flour
1 tsp baking powder
50 g/2 oz butter or block
    margarine, diced
200 g/7 oz soft light brown sugar
1 large egg, beaten
$1/2$ tsp vanilla extract

For the icing:

25 g/1 oz unsalted butter
5 tbsp soft light brown sugar
4 tbsp double cream

1

1

2

Shaggy Coconut Cupcakes

1 Preheat the oven to 180°C/350°F/Gas Mark 4. Line a 12-hole deep muffin tray with paper cases.

2 Sift the baking powder and flour into a large bowl. Add all the remaining ingredients and beat for about 2 minutes until smooth and creamy. Divide evenly between the paper cases.

3 Bake for 18–20 minutes until risen, golden and firm to the touch. Leave in the muffin trays for 2 minutes, then turn out to cool on a wire rack.

4 To decorate the cupcakes, if you are using the coconut liqueur, beat this into the buttercream and then swirl over each cupcake. To decorate, press large strands of shredded coconut into the buttercream. Keep for up to 3 days in an airtight container in a cool place.

Ingredients
MAKES 12

½ tsp baking powder
200 g/7 oz self-raising flour
175 g/6 oz caster sugar
2 tbsp desiccated coconut
175 g/6 oz soft margarine
3 medium eggs, beaten
2 tbsp milk

To decorate:
1 batch buttercream (*see* page 18)
1 tbsp coconut liqueur (optional)
175 g/6 oz large shredded
   coconut strands

Coffee & Walnut Fudge Cupcakes

1 Preheat the oven to 200 C/400 F/Gas Mark 6. Line two 12-hole bun trays with 16–18 small foil cases, depending on the depth of the tray holes.

2 Stir the flour into a bowl and add the butter, sugar, eggs and syrup. Beat for about 2 minutes, then fold in the walnuts.

3 Spoon the mixture into the paper cases and bake for about 12–14 minutes until well risen and springy in the centre. Remove to a wire rack to cool.

4 Make the frosting by sifting the icing sugar into a bowl. Add the butter, coffee extract and 1 tablespoon hot water. Beat until light and fluffy, then place in a piping bag fitted with a star nozzle. Pipe a swirl on each cupcake and top with a walnut piece. Keep for 3–4 days in an airtight container in a cool place.

Ingredients
MAKES 16–18

125 g/4 oz self-raising flour
125 g/4 oz butter, softened
125 g/ 4 oz golden caster sugar
2 medium eggs, beaten
1 tbsp golden syrup
50 g/2 oz walnuts, finely chopped

To decorate:
225 g/8 oz golden icing sugar
125 g/4 oz unsalted butter, softened
2 tsp coffee extract
16–18 small walnut pieces

1

2

4

Madeleine Cupcakes

1 Preheat the oven to 180°C/350°F/Gas Mark 4. Line a 12-hole muffin tray with 10–12 paper cases, depending on the depth of the holes.

2 Sift the flour into a bowl and add the butter, sugar, eggs and extract. Beat for about 2 minutes until smooth, then spoon into the paper cases.

3 Bake in the centre of the oven for about 14–16 minutes until well risen and springy in the centre. Transfer to a wire rack to cool.

4 To decorate the cupcakes, warm the raspberry jam in a small pan or in the microwave oven in a heatproof dish on low for a few seconds. Brush the warmed jam over the top of each cupcake. Lightly coat the top of each cupcake with coconut, then finish with a halved cherry. Keep for up to 3 days in an airtight container.

Ingredients
MAKES 10–12

125 g/4 oz self-raising flour
125 g/4 oz butter, softened
125 g/4 oz golden caster sugar
2 medium eggs, beaten
1 tsp vanilla extract

To decorate:
4 tbsp seedless raspberry jam
65 g/2½ oz desiccated coconut
glacé cherries, halved

3

4

4

Lamington Cupcakes

1 Preheat the oven to 180˚C/350˚F/Gas Mark 4. Line a 12-hole muffin tray with deep paper cases.

2 Sift the flour into a bowl and add the butter, sugar, eggs and extract. Beat for about 2 minutes until smooth, then spoon into the paper cases.

3 Bake in the centre of the oven for about 18 minutes until well risen and springy in the centre. Transfer to a wire rack to cool.

4 To make the icing, place the caster sugar, cocoa powder and water in a large heavy-based pan.

5 Heat over a low heat until every grain of sugar has dissolved. Bring to the boil and then simmer for about 6 minutes, without stirring, until thickened into syrup. Pour into a bowl and use the syrup while it is still hot, as it will set as it cools.

6 Place the coconut into a large bowl. Dip the top of each cupcake into the hot chocolate syrup to coat the top, then dip in coconut, decorate and place on a tray to dry. Keep for 2–3 days in an airtight container.

Ingredients
MAKES 12

125 g/4 oz self-raising flour
125 g/4 oz butter, softened
125 g/4 oz golden caster sugar
2 medium eggs, beaten
1 tsp vanilla extract

To decorate:
350 g/12 oz caster sugar
1 tbsp cocoa powder
125 ml/4 fl oz water
65 g/2½ oz desiccated coconut
ready-made chocolate decorations

4

5

6

Mini Cupcakes

1 Preheat the oven to 190°C/375°F/Gas Mark 5. Line a 24-hole mini-muffin tray with mini paper muffin cases.

2 Put the sugar, butter and lemon zest in a large bowl and beat until light and fluffy. Beat in the eggs a little at a time, adding a teaspoon of flour with each addition. Fold in the rest of the flour and the lemon juice and mix until smooth.

3 Spoon into the mini muffin cases and bake for about 12 minutes until golden and risen. Transfer to a wire rack to cool.

4 To make the icing, beat the butter and vanilla extract together until light and fluffy, then gradually beat in the icing sugar and milk until a soft, easy-to-spread consistency has formed. Colour the icing in batches with paste food colourings, then spread over the cold cupcakes with a flat-bladed knife. Decorate with sugar sprinkles. Keep in an airtight container for up to 2 days.

Ingredients
MAKES 24

100 g/3½ oz golden caster sugar
100 g/3½ oz butter, softened
finely grated zest of ½ lemon and
    1 tsp juice
2 medium eggs, beaten
100 g/3½ oz self-raising flour

To decorate:

50 g/2 oz unsalted butter, softened
1 tsp vanilla extract
125 g/4 oz icing sugar, sifted
1 tbsp milk
paste food colourings
sugar sprinkles

Raspberry Butterfly Cupcakes

1   Preheat the oven to 190°C/375°F/Gas Mark 5. Line one or two bun trays with 12–14 paper cases, depending on the depth of the holes.

2   Place all the cupcake ingredients in a large bowl and beat with an electric mixer for about 2 minutes until smooth. Fill the paper cases halfway up with the mixture.

3   Bake for about 15 minutes until firm, risen and golden. Remove to a wire rack to cool.

4   When cold, cut a small circle out of the top of each cupcake and then cut the circle in half to form wings.

5   Fill each cupcake with a teaspoon of raspberry jam. Replace the wings at an angle and top each with a fresh raspberry. Dust lightly with icing sugar and serve immediately.

Ingredients
MAKES 12–14

125 g/4 oz caster sugar
125 g/4 oz soft tub margarine
2 medium eggs
125 g/4 oz self-raising flour
$\frac{1}{2}$ tsp baking powder
$\frac{1}{2}$ tsp vanilla extract

To decorate:
4 tbsp seedless raspberry jam
12–14 fresh raspberries
icing sugar, to dust

3

4

5

Strawberry Swirl Cupcakes

1 Preheat the oven to 190°C/375°F/Gas Mark 5. Line a muffin tray with 12 deep paper cases.

2 Place all the cupcake ingredients except the jam in a large bowl and beat with an electric mixer for about 2 minutes until smooth. Fill the paper cases halfway up with the mixture.

3 Add ½ teaspoon jam to each case and swirl it into the mixture. Bake for about 15 minutes until firm, risen and golden. Remove to a wire rack to cool.

4 To prepare the frosting, beat the butter until soft, then gradually add the icing sugar until the mixture is light. Add the cream cheese and whisk until light and fluffy.

5 Divide the mixture in half and beat the strawberry jam and pink food colouring into one half. Fit a piping bag with a wide star nozzle and spoon strawberry cream on one side of the bag and the plain cream on the other. Pipe swirls on top of the cupcakes. Keep for up to 3 days in an airtight container in a cool place.

Ingredients
MAKES 12

125 g/4 oz caster sugar
125 g/4 oz soft tub margarine
2 medium eggs
125 g/4 oz self-raising flour
½ tsp baking powder
2 tbsp sieved strawberry jam

To decorate:
50 g/2 oz unsalted butter, softened
300 g/11 oz icing sugar, sifted
125 g/4 oz full-fat cream cheese
1 tbsp sieved strawberry jam
pink food colouring

Double Cherry Cupcakes

1 Preheat the oven to 190°C/375°F/Gas Mark 5. Line a 12-hole muffin tray with deep paper cases, or two trays with 18 fairy-cake cases. Wash the cherries, dry on absorbent kitchen paper and chop.

2 Dust the chopped glacé cherries lightly in a tablespoon of the flour, then mix with the morello cherries and set aside. Sift the rest of the flour into a bowl, then add the margarine, sugar, eggs and almond extract. Beat for about 2 minutes until smooth, then fold in the cherries.

3 Spoon the batter into the paper cases and bake for 15–20 minutes until well risen and springy in the centre. Turn out to cool on a wire rack.

4 To decorate the cupcakes, trim the tops level. Mix the icing sugar with 2–3 teaspoons warm water and a few drops pink food colouring to make a thick consistency. Spoon the icing over each cupcake, filling right up to the edge.

5 Chop the cherries finely and sprinkle over the icing. Leave to set for 30 minutes. Keep for up to 3 days in an airtight container.

Ingredients

MAKES 12 LARGE CUPCAKES
OR 18 FAIRY CAKES

50 g/2 oz glacé cherries
125 g/4 oz self-raising flour
25 g/1 oz dried morello cherries
125 g/4 oz soft margarine
125 g/4 oz caster sugar
2 medium eggs
1/2 tsp almond extract

To decorate:

125 g/4 oz fondant icing sugar
pale pink liquid food colouring
40 g/1 1/2 oz glacé cherries

Lemon & Ginger Cupcakes

1 Preheat the oven to 180°C/350°F/Gas Mark 4. Line two shallow muffin trays with 18 paper cases.

2 Place the syrup and margarine in a heavy-based pan and melt together gently.

3 Sift the flour and ginger into a bowl, then stir in the sultanas and sugar. Warm the milk and stir in the bicarbonate of soda.

4 Pour the syrup mixture, milk and beaten egg into the dry ingredients and beat until smooth. Pour the mixture into a jug.

5 Carefully spoon 2 tbsp of the mixture into each case (the mixture will be wet). Bake for about 30 minutes. Cool in the tins for 10 minutes, then turn out to cool on a wire rack.

6 To decorate, blend the icing sugar with the lemon juice and 1 tbsp warm water to make a thin glacé icing. Drizzle over the top of each cupcake, then top with glacé ginger pieces. Leave to set for 30 minutes. Keep in an airtight container for up to 5 days.

Ingredients

MAKES 18

8 tbsp golden syrup
125 g/4 oz block margarine
225 g/8 oz plain flour
2 tsp ground ginger
75 g/3 oz sultanas
50 g/2 oz soft dark brown sugar
200 ml/7 fl oz milk
1 tsp bicarbonate of soda
1 medium egg, beaten

To decorate:

125 g/4 oz golden icing sugar
1 tsp lemon juice
glacé ginger pieces

Crystallised Violet Cupcakes

1 Preheat the oven to 180°C/350°F/Gas Mark 4 and line a 12-hole muffin tray with deep paper cases.

2 Place the butter, sugar and eggs in a bowl. Sift in the flour and baking powder. Finely grate in the zest from the lemon.

3 Beat together for about 2 minutes with an electric hand mixer until pale and fluffy. Spoon into the paper cases and bake for 20–25 minutes until firm and golden. Cool on a wire rack.

4 To decorate the cupcakes, spread the violets on some nonstick baking parchment. Beat the egg white until frothy, then brush thinly over the violets. Dust with caster sugar and leave to dry out for 2 hours.

5 Beat the icing sugar with the colouring and enough water to give a thin coating consistency. Drizzle over the top of each cupcake quickly and top with a violet. Leave to set for 30 minutes. Store in an airtight container in a cool place. Keep for up to 2 days.

Ingredients
MAKES 12

150 g/5 oz butter, softened
150 g/5 oz caster sugar
3 medium eggs, beaten
150 g/5 oz self-raising flour
½ tsp baking powder
1 lemon

To decorate:
12 fresh violets
1 egg white
caster sugar, for dusting
125 g/4 oz fondant icing sugar
pale violet food colouring

Cream Cheese Pastel Swirls

1 Preheat the oven to 180°C/350°F/Gas Mark 4. Line a 12-hole muffin tray with deep paper cases.

2 Place the butter and sugar in a bowl and cream together. In another bowl, beat the eggs with the vanilla extract.

3 Sift the flour into the creamed mixture, then beat in the eggs until smooth. Spoon into the cases, filling them three-quarters full.

4 Bake for about 18 minutes until firm to the touch in the centre. Turn out to cool on a wire rack.

5 Divide the frosting into three batches. Colour one green and one pink with dots of food colouring and leave one batch plain. Place each batch in a piping bag fitted with a star nozzle and pipe large swirls on top of each cupcake. Keep for up to 3 days in an airtight container in a cool place.

Ingredients
MAKES 12

150 g/5 oz butter, softened
150 g/5 oz caster sugar
3 medium eggs
1 tsp vanilla extract
175 g/6 oz self-raising flour

To decorate:
1 batch cream cheese frosting
(see page 18)
paste food colourings

2

3

5

Daisy Chain Lemon Cupcakes

1 Preheat the oven to 190°C/375°F/Gas Mark 5. Line a bun tray with 12 paper cases.

2 Place all the cupcake ingredients in a large bowl and beat with an electric mixer for about 2 minutes until smooth. Fill the paper cases halfway up with the mixture.

3 Bake for about 15 minutes until firm, risen and golden. Remove to a wire rack to cool.

4 Roll out the icing thinly and stamp out small daisies with a fluted daisy cutter. Pipe a small yellow dot of icing into the centre of each and leave to dry out for 1 hour.

5 Blend the fondant icing sugar with a little water and a few dots of yellow colouring to make a thick, easy-to-spread icing, then smooth over the top of each cupcake. Decorate with the cut-out daisies immediately and leave to set for 1 hour. Keep for up to 3 days in an airtight container.

Ingredients
MAKES 12

125 g/4 oz caster sugar
125 g/4 oz soft tub margarine
2 medium eggs
125 g/4 oz self-raising flour
$\frac{1}{2}$ tsp baking powder
1 tsp lemon juice

To decorate:
50 g/2 oz ready-to-roll sugarpaste
yellow piping icing tube
225 g/8 oz fondant icing sugar
lemon yellow food colouring

Florentine-topped Cupcakes

1 Preheat the oven to 180˚C/350˚F/Gas Mark 4. Line two 12-hole muffin trays with 18 paper cases.

2 Place the butter and sugar in a bowl, then sift in the flour. In another bowl, beat the eggs with the vanilla extract, then add to the first mixture and beat until smooth.

3 Fold in half the cherries, angelica, peel and cranberries. Spoon into the cases, filling them three-quarters full.

4 Bake for about 18 minutes until firm to the touch in the centre. Turn out to cool on a wire rack.

5 Spoon a little melted chocolate on top of each cupcake, then scatter the remaining cherries, angelica, peel and cranberries and the almonds into the wet chocolate. Drizzle the remaining chocolate over the fruit topping with a teaspoon and leave to set for 30 minutes. Keep for up to 2 days in an airtight container.

Ingredients
MAKES 18

150 g/5 oz butter, softened
150 g/5 oz caster sugar
175 g/6 oz self-raising flour
3 medium eggs
1 tsp vanilla extract
75 g/3 oz glacé cherries, chopped
50 g/2 oz angelica, chopped
50 g/2 oz candied peel, chopped
50 g/2 oz dried cranberries

To decorate:
75 g/3 oz plain or milk
   chocolate, melted
50 g/2 oz flaked almonds

Fondant Fancies

1   Preheat the oven to 180°C/350°F/Gas Mark 4. Line two 12-hole bun trays with 16–18 paper cases, depending on the depth of the tray holes.

2   Sift the flour into a bowl and stir in the caster sugar and almonds. Add the butter, eggs and milk and beat until smooth.

3   Spoon into the paper cases and bake for 15–20 minutes until golden and firm to the touch. Turn out to cool on a wire rack. When cool, trim the tops flat if they have peaked slightly.

4   To decorate the cupcakes, make the fondant icing to a thick coating consistency, following the packet instructions. Divide into batches and colour each separately with a little paste food colouring. Keep each bowl covered with a damp cloth until needed. Spoon some icing over each cupcake, being sure to flood it right to the edge. Top each with a fancy decoration and leave to set for 30 minutes. Keep for up to 2 days in a cool place.

Ingredients
MAKES 16–18

150 g/5 oz self-raising flour
150 g/5 oz caster sugar
50 g/2 oz ground almonds
150 g/5 oz butter, softened
3 medium eggs, beaten
4 tbsp milk

To decorate:
450 g/1 lb fondant icing sugar
paste food colourings
selection fancy cake decorations

Lemon & Cardamom Cupcakes with Mascarpone Topping

1 Preheat the oven to 180°C/350°F/Gas Mark 4. Line a 12-hole muffin tray with deep paper cases. Crush the cardamom seeds and remove the outer cases. Melt the butter and leave aside to cool.

2 Sift the flours and baking powder into a bowl and stir in the crushed seeds, sugar and lemon zest.

3 In another bowl, whisk together the eggs and yogurt. Pour into the dry ingredients with the cooled melted butter and beat until combined.

4 Divide half the mixture between the paper cases, put a teaspoon of lemon curd into each, then top with the remaining mixture. Bake for about 25 minutes until golden.

5 To make the topping, beat the mascarpone with the icing sugar and lemon juice. Swirl onto each cupcake and top with lemon strips. Eat fresh on day of baking once decorated or store, undecorated, in an airtight container for up to 2 days and add the topping just before serving.

Ingredients
MAKES 12

1 tsp cardamom seeds
200 g/7 oz butter
50 g/2 oz plain flour
200 g/7 oz self-raising flour
1 tsp baking powder
200 g/7 oz caster sugar
zest of 1 lemon, finely grated
3 medium eggs
100 ml/3½ fl oz natural yogurt
4 tbsp lemon curd

To decorate:
250 g/9 oz tub mascarpone
6 tbsp icing sugar
1 tsp lemon juice
lemon zest strips

Almond & Cherry Cupcakes

1 Preheat the oven to 190°C/375°F/Gas Mark 5. Line a 12-hole bun tray with small paper cases. Wash the glacé cherries, then dry them thoroughly. Chop the cherries, then dust lightly in flour and set aside.

2 Sift the flour into a bowl, then add the margarine, sugar, eggs and extract. Beat until smooth for about 2 minutes, then fold in the chopped cherries.

3 Spoon into the paper cases. Bake for 15–20 minutes until golden and springy in the centre. Turn out to cool on a wire rack.

4 To decorate, mix the icing sugar with the lemon juice and 2 tsp water to form a smooth glacé icing. Add a little pink food colouring and drizzle over the top of each cupcake. Place a halved cherry on top and leave to set for 30 minutes. Keep for 2–3 days in an airtight container.

Ingredients

MAKES 12

50 g/2 oz glacé cherries, plus extra for decoration
125 g/4 oz self-raising flour, plus extra for dusting
125 g/4 oz soft margarine
125 g/4 oz caster sugar
2 medium eggs
1/2 tsp almond extract

To decorate:

125 g/4 oz icing sugar
1 tsp lemon juice
pink food colouring

Pink Butterfly Cupcakes

1 Preheat the oven to 180°C/350°F/Gas Mark 4 and line a 12-hole muffin tray with deep paper cases.

2 Place the butter, sugar, eggs and vanilla extract in a bowl and then sift in the flour and baking powder. Beat together for about 2 minutes with an electric hand mixer until pale and fluffy. Spoon into the paper cases and bake for 20–25 minutes until firm and golden. Cool on a wire rack.

3 To decorate the cupcakes, colour 200 g/7 oz of the sugarpaste pale pink and colour the remainder brown. Roll out the sugarpaste thinly and, using a cutter, template or freehand, cut out four petal shapes for the wings for each cupcake and set them on nonstick baking parchment or clingfilm. Cut out 48 shapes altogether and leave to dry flat until firm (about 2 hours). Colour the cream cheese frosting bright pink and place in a piping bag fitted with a star nozzle.

4 Pipe a swirl of pink icing to cover the top of each cupcake and then press four wings on top of each. Mould the brown icing into a thin body shape and place on each cupcake. Pipe dots on the wings with tubes of gel writing icing. Keep for up to 2 days in an airtight container in a cool place.

Ingredients
MAKES 12

150 g/5 oz butter, softened
150 g/5 oz caster sugar
3 medium eggs, beaten
1 tsp vanilla extract
150 g/5 oz self-raising flour
1/2 tsp baking powder

To decorate:

pink and brown paste food colouring
225 g/8 oz ready-to-roll sugarpaste
1 batch cream cheese frosting
   (see page 18)
tubes of gel writing icing

Indulgent Chocolate

The epitome of indulgence, chocolate deserves its own section. The perfect partner for fellow decadents such as fudge and toffee, it renders Chocolate Fudge Flake Muffins and Chocolate & Toffee Cupcakes to die for. Then there are the fruits and flavourings that give chocolate a different identity – why not try Mint Choc Chip or Chocolate & Orange Marbled Muffins? Of course, sometimes you just crave pure, unadulterated heaven, which you will find in Very Rich Chocolate Cupcakes.

Chocolate Mud Cupcakes

1 Preheat the oven to 190°C/375°F/Gas Mark 5. Line one or two bun trays with 16 foil or paper cases.

2 Place the butter, caster sugar and eggs in a large bowl and then sift in the flour and cocoa powder. Whisk together for about 2 minutes until smooth, then spoon into the cases, filling them two-thirds full.

3 Bake for about 14 minutes until well risen and springy to the touch. Cool on a wire rack.

4 To make the frosting, break the chocolate into squares and melt in a heatproof bowl over a pan of barely simmering water. Set aside to cool. Beat the butter and icing sugar together until fluffy, then whisk in the cooled melted chocolate. Swirl over the cupcakes with a flat-bladed knife. Scatter over the sprinkles. Keep for up to 3 days in a cool place.

Ingredients

MAKES 16

150 g/5 oz butter, softened
150 g/5 oz golden caster sugar
3 medium eggs, beaten
125 g/4 oz self-raising flour
25 g/1 oz cocoa powder

To decorate:

75 g/3 oz milk chocolate
75 g/3 oz unsalted butter, softened
150 g/5 oz golden icing sugar, sifted
white and dark chocolate sprinkles

White Chocolate Cupcakes

1 Preheat the oven to 180°C/350°F/Gas Mark 4. Line a 12-hole deep muffin tray with paper cases. Melt the butter and leave aside to cool.

2 Coarsely grate or chop the white chocolate. Sift the flours and baking powder into a bowl and stir in the sugar, lemon zest and chopped white chocolate.

3 In another bowl, whisk together the eggs and yogurt. Pour into the dry ingredients with the cooled melted butter and beat until combined. Spoon into the paper cases and bake for about 25 minutes until firm and golden.

4 To decorate the cupcakes, melt one quarter of the white chocolate in a heatproof bowl standing over a pan of barely simmering water. Spread the melted chocolate out onto a clean plastic board. When almost set, make into curls by pulling a sharp knife through the chocolate (*see* pages 21 and 76). Refrigerate for 30 minutes to set.

5 Melt the remaining white chocolate, then spoon over the cupcakes and leave for about 10 minutes until cooled and half set. Top each cupcake while still wet with the white chocolate curls and leave to set for 30 minutes. Keep for up to 2 days in the refrigerator.

Ingredients

MAKES 12

200 g/7 oz butter
125 g/4 oz white chocolate
50 g/2 oz plain flour
200 g/7 oz self-raising flour
1 tsp baking powder
200 g/7 oz caster sugar
finely grated zest of ½ lemon
3 medium eggs
100 ml/3½ fl oz natural yogurt
250 g/9 oz white chocolate,
    chopped, to decorate

4

4

5

Double Chocolate Chip Cupcakes

1 Preheat the oven to 180°C/350°F/Gas Mark 4. Line one or two bun trays with 14 small paper cases.

2 Place the margarine and sugar in a large bowl with the eggs and sift in the cocoa powder, flour and baking powder. Beat for about 2 minutes until smooth, then fold in the chocolate chips with the milk.

3 Spoon into the paper cases and bake for 15–20 minutes until firm. Place on a wire rack to cool. Keep for 4–5 days in an airtight container.

Ingredients
MAKES 14

125 g/4 oz soft margarine
125g/4 oz golden caster sugar
2 medium eggs, beaten
25 g/1 oz cocoa powder
175 g/6 oz self-raising flour
1 tsp baking powder
50 g/2 oz milk chocolate chips
50 g/2 oz dark or white
    chocolate chips
1 tbsp milk

Chocolate Fudge Flake Cupcakes

1 Preheat the oven to 180°C/350°F/Gas Mark 4. Line a 12-hole muffin tray with deep paper cases, or one or two bun trays with 18 fairy-cake cases.

2 Sift the flour and cocoa powder into a large bowl, add the margarine, sugar, eggs and milk and whisk with an electric beater for about 2 minutes until smooth.

3 Divide the mixture between the paper cases and bake for about 20 minutes for the larger cupcakes and 15 minutes for the fairy cakes until a skewer inserted into the middle comes out clean. Turn out to cool on a wire rack.

4 To make the topping, melt the butter with the syrup and cocoa powder in a pan. Cool, then whisk in the icing sugar until the mixture has thickened, and beat in the cream cheese. Spread the frosting over the cupcakes. Chop the flake bars into small chunks, then place one chunk in the centre of each cupcake. Keep for 2–3 days in the refrigerator.

Ingredients

MAKES 12 LARGE CUPCAKES
OR 18 FAIRY CAKES

125 g/4 oz self-raising flour
25 g/1 oz cocoa powder
125 g/4 oz soft margarine
125 g/4 oz soft light brown sugar
2 medium eggs, beaten
2 tbsp milk

To decorate:

25 g/1 oz butter
50 g/2 oz golden syrup
15 g/¹/₂ oz cocoa powder
125 g/4 oz golden icing sugar
25 g/1 oz cream cheese
40 g/1¹/₂ oz chocolate flake bars

Black Forest Cupcakes

1 Preheat the oven to 180°C/350°F/Gas Mark 4. Line a 12-hole muffin tray with large paper cases, or one or two bun trays with 24 small paper cases. Blend the cocoa powder with the boiling water and leave to cool.

2 Sift the flour and baking powder into a bowl and add the margarine, sugar, eggs, milk and the cocoa mixture. Whisk together for about 2 minutes until smooth, then spoon into the paper cases.

3 Bake for 15–20 minutes until springy to the touch. Cool in the trays for 5 minutes, then turn out onto a wire rack to cool.

4 To decorate the cupcakes, melt the chocolate and spread it out to cool on a clean plastic board. When it is almost set, pull a sharp knife through the chocolate to make curls. Refrigerate these until needed.

5 Brush the top of each cupcake with a little raspberry jam. Whisk the cream until it forms soft peaks, then fold in the kirsch, if using. Pipe or swirl the cream on top of each cupcake. Top with chocolate curls and whole glacé cherries for the large muffins or halved cherries for the smaller ones. Eat fresh or keep for 1 day in the refrigerator.

Ingredients
MAKES 12 LARGE CUPCAKES
OR 24 SMALL CUPCAKES

1 tbsp cocoa powder
2 tbsp boiling water
175 g/6 oz self-raising flour
1 tsp baking powder
125 g/4 oz soft tub margarine
175 g/6 oz soft dark brown sugar
2 medium eggs
3 tbsp milk

To decorate:
125 g/4 oz dark chocolate
4 tbsp seedless raspberry
  jam, warmed
150 ml/¼ pint double cream
1 tbsp kirsch (optional)
12 natural-coloured glacé cherries

4

5

5

Mocha Cupcakes

1 Preheat the oven to 180°C/350°F/Gas Mark 4. Line a 12-hole muffin tray with deep paper cases.

2 Place the margarine and sugar in a large bowl, then sift in the flour and cocoa powder.

3 In another bowl, beat the eggs with the syrup, then add to the cocoa mixture. Whisk everything together with the milk using an electric beater for 2 minutes, or by hand with a wooden spoon until smooth.

4 Divide the mixture between the cases, filling them three-quarters full. Bake for about 20 minutes until the centres are springy to the touch and a skewer inserted ino the centre comes out clean. Turn out to cool on a wire rack.

5 Make the frosting by sifting the icing sugar into a bowl. Add the butter, coffee extract and 1 tbsp hot water. Beat until fluffy, then swirl onto each cupcake with a flat-bladed knife. Top each with a fresh cape gooseberry. Keep for up to 2 days in a cool place.

Ingredients
MAKES 12

125 g/4 oz soft margarine
125 g/4 oz golden caster sugar
150 g/5 oz self-raising flour
2 tbsp cocoa powder
2 medium eggs
1 tbsp golden syrup
2 tbsp milk

To decorate:
225 g/8 oz golden icing sugar
125 g/4 oz unsalted butter, softened
2 tsp coffee extract
12 cape gooseberries, papery
    covering pulled back

Chocolate & Cranberry Cupcakes

1 Preheat the oven to 180°C/350°F/Gas Mark 4. Line a muffin tray with 12 deep paper cases.

2 Place the margarine, sugar and eggs in a bowl, then sift in the flour, cocoa powder and baking powder.

3 Add the milk and beat until smooth, then fold in the chocolate chips and cranberries. Spoon into the paper cases and bake for 15–20 minutes until firm in the centre. Remove to a wire rack to cool.

4 To decorate the cupcakes, blend the cocoa powder with 1 tablespoon hot water until smooth. Cool for 5 minutes. Beat the butter and icing sugar together and then beat in the cocoa mixture.

5 Place in a piping bag with a plain nozzle and pipe swirls on top of each cupcake. Top with dried cranberries. Keep for 2–3 days in the refrigerator.

Ingredients
MAKES 12

125 g/4 oz soft margarine
125 g/4 oz golden caster sugar
2 medium eggs
175 g/6 oz self-raising flour
25 g/1 oz cocoa powder
1 tsp baking powder
2 tbsp milk
125 g/4 oz milk chocolate chips
50 g/2 oz dried cranberries

To decorate:
25 g/1 oz cocoa powder
40 g/1½ oz unsalted butter
125 g/4 oz golden icing sugar
25 g/1 oz dried cranberries

2

3

3

Rocky Road Cupcakes

1 Preheat the oven to 180°C/350°F/Gas Mark 4. Line two bun trays with 14–18 paper cases or silicone cupcake moulds, depending on the depth of the holes.

2 Sift the flour and cocoa powder into a large bowl. Add the sugar, margarine, eggs and milk and whisk with an electric beater for about 2 minutes until smooth.

3 Divide the mixture evenly between the paper cases and bake for about 20 minutes until a skewer inserted into the middle comes out clean. Remove the tray from the oven, but leave the oven on.

4 To make the topping, gently melt the chocolate and butter together in a small pan over a low heat. Place the melted chocolate mixture in an icing bag made of greaseproof paper and snip away the end. Pipe a little of the mixture on top of each cupcake, then scatter the marshmallows and nuts over each one and return to the oven. Bake for 2–3 minutes to soften the marshmallows. Remove from the oven and pipe the remaining chocolate over the marshmallows. Leave to cool in the trays for 5 minutes, then remove to cool on a wire rack. Serve warm or cold. Keep for up to 2 days in an airtight container.

Ingredients
MAKES 14–18

125 g/4 oz self-raising flour
25 g/1 oz cocoa powder
125 g/4 oz soft dark brown sugar
125 g/4 oz soft margarine
2 medium eggs, beaten
2 tbsp milk

To decorate:
75 g/3 oz dark chocolate, broken into squares
40 g/1½ oz butter
75 g/3 oz mini marshmallows
40 g/1½ oz chopped mixed nuts

Chocolate & Orange Marbled Muffins

1 Preheat the oven to 180°C/350°F/Gas Mark 4. Grease two deep 6-hole muffin trays, or line with 10–12 deep paper cases, depending on the depth of the holes.

2 Put the margarine, sugar, eggs, flour and baking powder into a large mixing bowl. Whisk the mixture together for about 2 minutes until smooth.

3 Place half the mixture into another bowl and sift over the cocoa powder, then stir in until blended. Stir the orange juice and zest into the other mixture.

4 Spoon the cocoa mixture evenly between the prepared tins. Spoon over the orange mixture and, using a flat-bladed knife, swirl through the two mixtures to make a marbled pattern.

5 Bake for 15–20 minutes until well risen and firm to the touch. Cool in the trays for 5 minutes, then turn out to cool on a wire rack. While still warm, drizzle each muffin with a little clear honey. Keep for up to 4 days in an airtight container.

Ingredients

MAKES 10–12

175 g/6 oz soft margarine
175 g/6 oz caster sugar
3 medium eggs
175 g/6 oz self-raising flour
1 tsp baking powder
1 tbsp cocoa powder
finely grated zest and juice of
    ½ orange
4 tbsp clear honey, to glaze

Mint Choc Chip Cupcakes

1 Preheat the oven to 180°C/350°F/Gas Mark 4. Line a 12-hole muffin tray with deep paper cases.

2 Place the margarine, sugar and eggs in a bowl, then sift in the flour, cocoa powder and baking powder. Beat by hand or with an electric mixer until smooth, then fold in the chocolate chips and the crushed mints.

3 Spoon the mixture into the paper cases and bake for 15–20 minutes until firm in the centre. Remove to a wire rack to cool.

4 Beat the butter and icing sugar together with 1 tbsp warm water, the peppermint extract and the food colouring. Place in a piping bag with a star nozzle and pipe swirls on top of each cupcake. Cut the chocolate into triangles and place one on top of each cake. Keep for 3–4 days in an airtight container in a cool place.

Ingredients
MAKES 12

125 g/4 oz soft margarine
125 g/4 oz golden caster sugar
2 medium eggs
175 g/6 oz self-raising flour
25 g/1 oz cocoa powder
1 tsp baking powder
75 g/3 oz dark chocolate chips
25 g/1 oz clear hard peppermint
    sweets, crushed into crumbs

To decorate:
50 g/2 oz unsalted butter
175 g/6 oz icing sugar
peppermint flavouring or extract
green food colouring
50 g/2 oz chocolate squares

Chocolate & Toffee Cupcakes

1 Preheat the oven to 180 C/350 F/Gas Mark 4. Line one or two bun trays with 12–14 paper cases, depending on the depth of the holes. Cut one quarter of the fudge into slices for decoration. Chop the rest into small cubes. Set all the fudge aside.

2 Place the margarine and the sugar in a large bowl and then sift in the flour and cocoa powder. In another bowl, beat the eggs with the syrup, then add to the flour mixture. Whisk together with an electric beater for 2 minutes, or by hand with a wooden spoon until smooth. Gently fold in the fudge cubes.

3 Spoon the mixture into the cases, filling them three-quarters full. Bake for about 15 minutes until a skewer inserted into the centre comes out clean. Turn out to cool on a wire rack.

4 Swirl the cream cheese frosting over each cupcake, then finish by topping with a fudge slice. Keep for 3–4 days chilled in a sealed container.

Ingredients
MAKES 12–14

125 g/4 oz soft fudge
125 g/4 oz soft margarine
125 g/4 oz golden caster sugar
150 g/5 oz self-raising flour
2 tbsp cocoa powder
2 medium eggs
1 tbsp golden syrup
1 batch cream cheese frosting
   (see page 18), to decorate

1

3

4

Chocolate, Banana & Pecan Muffins

1 Preheat the oven to 180˚C/350˚F/Gas Mark 4. Grease or line one or two deep 12-hole muffin trays with 12–14 deep paper cases, depending on the depth of the holes. Mash the bananas in a bowl.

2 In another bowl, whisk the butter and sugar together. Add the mashed bananas, eggs and vanilla extract. Sift in the cinnamon, flour, cocoa powder, baking powder and bicarbonate of soda. Add the buttermilk and fold in with the chopped nuts.

3 Spoon the mixture into the cases. Bake for 25 minutes until well risen and firm in the centre. Cool on a wire rack.

4 To decorate the muffins, put the granulated sugar in a small pan with 5 tbsp cold water. Heat gently until every grain of sugar has dissolved, then simmer until the mixture turns golden. Holding the pan away from you, as the mixture may spit, add the cream and 1 tbsp water and then stir in the nuts. Remove the pan from the heat to cool slightly.

5 In a bowl, beat the cream cheese with the icing sugar and swirl on top of the muffins. Drizzle with the warm caramel nut sauce and leave to set. Keep for 2–3 days chilled in a sealed container.

Ingredients

MAKES 12–14

125 g/4 oz butter, softened
225 g/8 oz soft light brown sugar
250 g/9 oz ripe bananas, peeled
2 medium eggs
1 tsp vanilla extract
½ tsp ground cinnamon
225 g/8 oz plain flour
25 g/1 oz cocoa powder, sifted
1 tsp baking powder
1 tsp bicarbonate of soda
85 ml/3 fl oz buttermilk
50 g/2 oz pecan nuts, chopped

To decorate:

150 g/5 oz granulated sugar
4 tbsp double cream
50 g/2 oz pecan nuts, chopped
225 g/8 oz cream cheese
125 g/4 oz golden icing sugar

Cappuccino Cupcakes

1 Preheat the oven to 180°C/350°F/Gas Mark 4. Line one or two bun trays with 12–14 paper cases or silicone moulds, depending on the depth of the holes.

2 Place the margarine and the sugar in a large bowl, then sift in the flour and cocoa powder.

3 In another bowl, beat the eggs with the syrup, then add to the flour mixture. Whisk together with an electric beater for 2 minutes, or by hand with a wooden spoon, until smooth and then fold in the grated chocolate.

4 Divide the mixture between the cases, filling them three-quarters full. Bake for about 20 minutes until springy to the touch in the centre. Turn out to cool on a wire rack.

5 To decorate, whisk the cream until it forms soft peaks, then whisk in the coffee extract. Swirl over the tops of the muffins with a small palette knife. Scatter the tops with chocolate sprinkles to serve. Eat on the day of decorating or keep for 1 day in a sealed container in the refrigerator.

Ingredients
MAKES 12–14

125 g/4 oz soft margarine
125 g/4 oz golden caster sugar
150 g/5 oz self-raising flour
2 tbsp cocoa powder
2 medium eggs
1 tbsp golden syrup
50 g/2 oz finely grated chocolate

To decorate:
150 ml/¼ pint double cream
½ tsp coffee extract
chocolate sprinkles

3

5

5

Mini Chocolate Ripple Muffins

1 Preheat the oven to 180°C/350°F/Gas Mark 4. Grease a 24-hole mini-muffin tray, or line with paper cases.

2 Put the margarine, sugar, eggs, flour and baking powder into a large mixing bowl. Whisk for about 2 minutes until smooth, then pour half the mixture into a separate bowl and sift the cocoa powder over it. Stir in the milk until blended. Stir the vanilla extract into the first mixture.

3 Spoon the vanilla mixture evenly between the prepared tins, then spoon over the cocoa mixture. Using a small spoon, swirl through the two mixtures to make a marbled pattern.

4 Bake for 12–15 minutes until well risen and firm to the touch. Cool in the trays for 5 minutes, then turn out to cool on a wire rack. Keep in an airtight container for 3–4 days.

Ingredients
MAKES 24

175 g/6 oz soft margarine
175 g/6 oz caster sugar
3 medium eggs
175 g/6 oz self-raising flour
1 tsp baking powder
1 tbsp cocoa powder
1 tbsp milk
1/2 tsp vanilla extract

Chunky Chocolate Cupcakes

1 Make the frosting first in order to allow it to cool. Place the sugar and evaporated milk in a heavy-based pan and stir over a low heat until every grain of sugar has dissolved. Simmer for 5 minutes, but do not allow the mixture to boil.

2 Remove the sugar mixture from the heat, cool for 5 minutes and then add the chocolate and butter. Stir until these melt. Pour the mixture into a bowl and chill for 2 hours until thickened.

3 Preheat the oven to 180˚C/350˚F/Gas Mark 4. Line one or two deep muffin trays with 12–14 paper cases, depending on the depth of the holes. Place the margarine and sugar in a bowl with the eggs and sift in the cocoa powder, flour and baking powder. Beat with the milk for about 2 minutes until smooth, then fold in the chopped chocolate.

4 Spoon into the paper cases and bake for 15–20 minutes until firm. Place on a wire rack to cool.

5 Remove the frosting from the fridge and beat to soften it slightly. Swirl it over the muffins. Keep in a cool place in a sealed container for 3–4 days.

Ingredients
MAKES 12–14

To decorate:
75 g/3 oz granulated sugar
5 tbsp evaporated milk
125 g/4 oz dark chocolate, chopped
40 g/1½ oz unsalted butter

To make the muffins:
125 g/4 oz soft margarine
125 g/4 oz golden caster sugar
2 medium eggs, beaten
25 g/1 oz cocoa powder
175 g/6 oz self-raising flour
1 tsp baking powder
2 tbsp milk
50 g/2 oz milk chocolate, chopped
50 g/2 oz dark or white
   chocolate, chopped

Chocolate Cupcakes with Irish Cream Topping

1 Preheat the oven to 180°C/350°F/Gas Mark 4. Line one or two muffin trays with 12–14 deep paper cases, depending on the depth of the holes.

2 Place the margarine and the sugar in a large bowl, then sift in the flour and cocoa powder. In another bowl, beat the eggs with the syrup and then add to the first bowl. Whisk together with an electric beater for 2 minutes, or by hand with a wooden spoon, until smooth.

3 Divide the mixture between the cases, filling them three-quarters full. Bake for about 20 minutes until the centre is springy to the touch. Turn out to cool on a wire rack.

4 For the decoration, whip the cream until it forms soft peaks. Gently fold in the cream liqueur, then place the mixture in a piping bag fitted with a plain nozzle. Pipe the cream in swirls, then top with chocolate sprinkles. Keep refrigerated in a sealed container until needed and eat within 2 days.

Ingredients
MAKES 12–14

125 g/4 oz soft margarine
125 g/4 oz golden caster sugar
150 g/5 oz self-raising flour
2 tbsp cocoa powder
2 medium eggs
1 tbsp golden syrup

To decorate:
150 ml/¼ pint double cream
2 tbsp Irish cream liqueur
chocolate sprinkles

Very Rich Chocolate Cupcakes

1 Preheat the oven to 190°C/375°F/Gas Mark 5. Line one or two 12-hole bun trays with 12–14 paper cases, depending on the depth of the holes.

2 Sift the flour and cocoa powder into a bowl and add the sugar, butter, eggs and milk. Whisk until smooth, then spoon into the paper cases.

3 Bake for about 14 minutes until just firm to the touch in the centre. Transfer to a wire rack to cool.

4 To decorate the cupcakes, break the chocolate into pieces and melt in a heatproof bowl standing over a pan of warm water.

5 In another pan, bring the cream to just below boiling, then remove from the heat and stir in the liquid glucose. Add the melted chocolate and stir until smooth and glossy. Spoon over the cupcakes and immediately top each with a chocolate decoration. Leave to set for 30 minutes. Keep for up to 3 days in an airtight container in a cool place.

Ingredients
MAKES 12–14

75 g/3 oz self-raising flour
25 g/1 oz cocoa powder
75 g/3 oz soft dark brown sugar
75 g/3 oz butter, softened
3 medium eggs
2 tbsp milk

To decorate:
200 g/7 oz dark chocolate
100 ml/3½ fl oz whipping cream
1 tbsp liquid glucose
selection chocolate decorations

4

5

5

Triple Chocolate Muffins

1 Preheat the oven to 180°C/350°F/Gas Mark 4. Line nine holes of a 12-hole muffin tray with deep paper cases.

2 Chop the dark chocolate into rough chunks and place in a small heavy-based pan with the milk and butter. Heat gently until the mixture melts together, then leave to cool.

3 Chop the milk and white chocolate coarsely and place in a mixing bowl. Sift in the flour and bicarbonate of soda, then stir in the soft light brown sugar.

4 In another bowl or jug, beat the egg with the yogurt, then add to the dry ingredients in the bowl with the cooled melted mixture and quickly mix together with a fork. Spoon into the cases and bake for about 25 minutes until risen and firm to the touch. Leave in the tray for 2 minutes to firm up and then turn out onto a wire rack to cool. Keep for up to 5 days in an airtight container.

Ingredients
MAKES 9

50 g/2 oz dark chocolate
1 tbsp milk
75 g/3 oz butter or block margarine
50 g/2 oz milk chocolate
50 g/2 oz white chocolate
200 g/7 oz self-raising flour
$\frac{1}{2}$ tsp bicarbonate of soda
125 g/4 oz soft light brown sugar
1 medium egg
150 ml/$\frac{1}{4}$ pint natural yogurt

Orange Drizzle Cupcakes

1 Preheat the oven to 190°C/375°F/Gas Mark 5. Grease 10 deep muffin moulds or line a 12-hole muffin tray with 10 deep paper cases.

2 Melt the chocolate in a heatproof bowl over a pan of warm water or in the microwave oven on low for 30 seconds and leave to cool.

3 Put the butter and sugar in a large bowl and whisk until light and fluffy. Gradually beat in the eggs, adding a teaspoon of flour with each addition. Beat in the cooled melted chocolate, then sift in the flour. Add the orange zest and yogurt to the bowl and whisk until smooth.

4 Spoon the mixture into the paper cases and bake for about 25 minutes until well risen and springy to the touch. Leave for 2 minutes in the moulds or tray, then turn out onto a wire rack.

5 To decorate, mix the orange zest and juice into the buttercream and use to fill a piping bag fitted with a star nozzle. Pipe swirls of buttercream on top of each cupcake. Warm the marmalade and place small drizzles over the cupcakes with a teaspoon. Keep in an airtight container in a cool place for 4 days.

Ingredients
MAKES 10

75 g/3 oz dark chocolate, chopped
125 g/4 oz butter
125 g/4 oz caster sugar
2 medium eggs, beaten
200 g/7 oz self-raising flour
zest of $\frac{1}{2}$ orange, finely grated
5 tbsp thick natural yogurt

To decorate:
finely grated zest and 1 tbsp juice
    from 1 small orange
1 batch buttercream (see page 18)
2 tbsp marmalade

Blondie Cupcakes

1 Preheat the oven to 180°C/350°F/Gas Mark 4. Line two muffin trays with 14 deep paper cases, or one mini-muffin tray with 24 paper cases. Roughly chop the pecan nuts and apricots.

2 Beat the butter with the sugar until light and fluffy, then add the eggs and vanilla extract gradually, beating between each addition. Sift the flour and baking powder into the bowl, then fold the white chocolate chips, nuts and apricots into the mixture, along with the milk, until evenly combined.

3 Spoon the mixture into the prepared tray(s). Bake for about 25 minutes until just firm. Leave in the tray(s) for 10 minutes, then turn out to cool on a wire rack.

4 Fill a small greaseproof paper icing bag with the melted chocolate and snip away the end. Pipe a drizzle pattern on top of the cupcakes and leave to set for 30 minutes. Keep in an airtight container for up to 5 days.

Ingredients

MAKES 14 LARGE
OR 24 MINI CUPCAKES

90 g/3¼ oz pecan nuts
90 g/3¼ oz ready-to-eat
    dried apricots
175 g/6 oz unsalted butter, softened
300 g/11 oz caster sugar
3 medium eggs, beaten
1 tsp vanilla extract
200 g/7 oz plain flour
1 tsp baking powder
100 g/3½ oz white chocolate chips
1 tbsp milk
50 g/2 oz white chocolate, melted,
    to decorate

Unbaked Chocolate Cupcakes

1 Wash eight ridged deep silicone moulds and dry them with kitchen paper to ensure they are completely free of moisture.

2 Break the chocolate into small pieces and place in a bowl. Set the bowl over a saucepan of warm water and heat the water to barely simmering to melt the chocolate, or place the bowl in the microwave and melt on low in bursts of 30 seconds.

3 When the chocolate has melted, brush it round the insides of the moulds with a teaspoon or pastry brush, making sure to go into all the ridges. Chill the moulds for 1 hour.

4 When the chocolate has set, brush on another thicker layer inside the cases and chill again. Once the cases are solid, carefully peel the silicone moulds away from the outsides.

5 Cut a cube of trifle sponge to fit inside a chocolate case, put inside the case and sprinkle the sponge with sherry or liqueur. Place a small or halved strawberry on top of this. Repeat with the remaining chocolate cases. Whip the cream until it forms soft peaks and place in a piping bag fitted with a large star nozzle. Pipe swirls into each case and top with another small or halved strawberry. Refrigerate until needed for up to 24 hours.

Ingredients
MAKES 8

For the cases:
450 g/1 lb dark chocolate

For the filling:
50 g/2 oz trifle sponges
2 tbsp sweet sherry or orange liqueur
350 g/12 oz strawberries
450 ml/³/₄ pint double cream

Celebrate & Party

Cupcakes are ideal for parties and celebrations, since they can be personalised and decorated in any way, and their individual form makes them easy for guests to pick up and consume, with no cutting necessary! From figurative designs ideal for kids' parties, such as Pirate Cupcakes, to beautiful and delicate designs for romantic and special occasions, such as Winter Wedding Cupcakes, you have a plethora of choices and a world of inspiration.

Banoffee Cupcakes

1 Preheat the oven to 180°C/350°F/Gas Mark 4. Line a 12-hole muffin tray with 10–12 deep paper cases, depending on the depth of the holes.

2 Peel and mash the bananas in a large bowl, then add the margarine, sugar, milk and eggs. Sift in the flour and baking powder and beat together for about 2 minutes until smooth.

3 Fold in 50 g/2 oz of the fudge pieces and then spoon the mixture into the paper cases. Bake for about 20 minutes until golden and firm. Remove from the baking trays to a wire rack to cool.

4 For the decoration, blend the icing sugar with 3–4 tsp cold water to make a thin icing. Drizzle over the top of each cupcake and, while the icing is still wet, top with the remaining mini fudge pieces and the banana flakes. Leave to dry out for 30 minutes to set the icing. Keep in an airtight container for up to 3 days.

Ingredients
MAKES 10–12

175 g/6 oz soft ripe bananas
125 g/4 oz soft margarine
75 g/3 oz golden caster sugar
1 tbsp milk
2 medium eggs
225 g/8 oz plain flour
1 tbsp baking powder
75 g/3 oz mini soft fudge pieces

To decorate:
125 g/4 oz golden icing sugar
10–12 semi-dried banana flakes

Sunflower Cupcakes

1 Preheat the oven to 180°C/350°F/Gas Mark 4 and line two bun trays with 18 paper fairy-cake cases.

2 Place the butter, sugar and beaten eggs in a bowl, then sift in the flour and baking powder. Finely grate the zest from the orange into the bowl and squeeze out 2 tbsp juice.

3 Beat together for about 2 minutes, preferably with an electric hand mixer, until pale and fluffy. Spoon the mixture into the paper cases and bake for about 15 minutes until firm and golden. Cool on a wire rack.

4 To decorate, colour three-quarters of the buttercream bright yellow and the remainder orange. Place in two piping bags fitted with star nozzles. Pipe a border of straight lines round the outer edges to form petals. Pipe more petals to fill in the centres. Pipe a circle of orange dots in the centre of each to finish. Keep for up to 3 days in a cool place.

Ingredients
MAKES 18

150 g/5 oz butter, softened
150 g/5 oz caster sugar
3 medium eggs, beaten
150 g/5 oz self-raising flour
$\frac{1}{2}$ tsp baking powder
zest and 2 tbsp juice from
    1 small orange

To decorate:
1 batch buttercream (see page 18)
yellow and orange food colourings

2

4

4

Boys' & Girls' Names

1 Preheat the oven to 180°C/350°F/Gas Mark 4. Line two 12-hole bun trays with 16–18 paper fairy-cake cases or silicone moulds, depending on the depth of the holes.

2 Sift the flour into a bowl and stir together with the caster sugar. Add the margarine, eggs and vanilla extract and beat together for about 2 minutes until smooth.

3 Spoon into the cases and bake for 15–20 minutes until golden and firm to the touch.

4 Turn out onto a wire rack. When cool, trim the tops flat if they have peaked slightly.

5 Divide the buttercream into batches and colour pink, green and yellow. Spread the icing over the cakes. Coat the edges of each fairy cake with brightly coloured sprinkles, then add a name in the centre of each one with the writing icing. Keep in an airtight container in a cool place for 2 days.

Ingredients
MAKES 16–18

175 g/6 oz self-raising flour
175 g/6 oz caster sugar
175 g/6 oz soft margarine
3 medium eggs, beaten
1 tsp vanilla extract

To decorate:
1 batch buttercream (see page 18)
paste food colourings
sprinkles and decorations
gel writing icing tubes

Pink Party Piggies

1   Preheat the oven to 190°C/375°F/Gas Mark 5. Line a bun tray with 12 small paper cases.

2   Place all the cupcake ingredients in a large bowl and beat with an electric mixer for about 2 minutes until smooth. Half-fill the paper cases with the mixture.

3   Bake for about 15 minutes until firm, risen and golden. Set on a wire rack to cool.

4   To decorate, mix the buttercream with the pink food colouring until it is pale pink. Spread smoothly over the top of each cupcake with a small palette knife. Cut a slice from a pink marshmallow with wetted scissors, then cut this into quarters to form the ears and press into the buttercream. Place a large halved marshmallow in the centre to form the snout. Add edible gold or silver balls to form eyes. Keep for 2–3 days sealed in an airtight container.

Ingredients
MAKES 12

125 g/4 oz caster sugar
125 g/4 oz soft tub margarine
2 medium eggs
1 tbsp milk
125 g/4 oz self-raising flour
1/2 tsp baking powder

To decorate:
1 batch buttercream (*see* page 18)
pink liquid food colouring
pink marshmallows
edible gold or silver balls

4

4

4

Teddy Bear Cupcakes

1 Preheat the oven to 180°C/350°F/Gas Mark 4. Line two 12-hole bun trays with 14–16 paper fairy-cake cases or silicone moulds, depending on the depth of the holes.

2 Sift the flour into a bowl and stir together with the caster sugar. Add the margarine, eggs and vanilla extract and beat together for about 2 minutes until smooth.

3 Spoon into the cases and bake for 15–20 minutes until golden and firm to the touch. Turn out on a wire rack. When cool, trim the tops flat if they have peaked slightly.

4 Colour the sugarpaste icing golden brown. Dust a small board with icing sugar. Roll the coloured sugarpaste thinly and cut out bear shapes. Leave to dry for 30 minutes.

5 Mix the fondant icing sugar with enough cold water to form a stiff shiny icing of coating consistency and colour this light brown. Flood the icing on top of each cupcake and, while still wet, place a bear shape onto each. Mix the royal icing sugar with a little water to make a stiff paste and then pipe on eyes, a nose, a mouth and buttons. Leave to set for 30 minutes. Keep for 1 day in an airtight container.

Ingredients
MAKES 14–16

125 g/4 oz self-raising flour
125 g/4 oz caster sugar
125 g/4 oz soft margarine
2 medium eggs, beaten
1 tsp vanilla extract

To decorate:
225 g/8 oz ready-to-roll sugarpaste
brown paste food colouring
325 g/11½ oz fondant icing sugar,
    plus extra for dusting
6 tbsp royal icing sugar

5

5

Kitty Faces Cupcakes

1 Preheat the oven to 180°C/350°F/Gas Mark 4. Line two 12-hole bun trays with 12–14 paper fairy-cake cases or silicone moulds, depending on the depth of the holes.

2 Sift the flour into a bowl and stir together with the caster sugar. Add the margarine, eggs and vanilla extract and beat together for about 2 minutes until smooth.

3 Spoon into the cases and bake for 15–20 minutes until golden and firm to the touch. Turn out on a wire rack. When cool, trim the tops flat if they have peaked slightly.

4 Colour the buttercream pink and spread over the top of each fairy cake. Pour the coconut onto a shallow dish. Press the top of each iced cupcake into the coconut. Cut the sweets to form pink ears, eyes, a jelly nose and whiskers and pipe on a red mouth in red gel icing. Keep in an airtight container in a cool place for 2 days.

Ingredients
MAKES 14–16

125 g/4 oz self-raising flour
125 g/4 oz caster sugar
125 g/4 oz soft margarine
2 medium eggs, beaten
1 tsp vanilla extract

To decorate:
1 batch buttercream (see page 18)
pink paste food colouring
50 g/2 oz desiccated coconut
liquorice allsorts sweets
red gel writing icing tube

Pirate Cupcakes

1 Preheat the oven to 180°C/350°F/Gas Mark 4. Line two 12-hole bun trays with 14–16 paper fairy-cake cases or silicone moulds, depending on the depth of the holes.

2 Sift the flour into a bowl and stir together with the caster sugar. Add the margarine, eggs and vanilla extract and beat together for about 2 minutes until smooth. Divide the mixture between the cases and bake for 15–20 minutes until golden and firm to the touch. Turn out on a wire rack. When cool, trim the tops flat if they have peaked slightly.

3 To decorate, lightly coat the top of each cupcake with a little buttercream. Colour three quarters of the sugarpaste pale pink and roll out thinly on a surface dusted with icing sugar. Stamp or cut out circles 6 cm/2½ inches wide and place these on the buttercream to cover the top of each cupcake.

4 Colour some of the remaining sugarpaste blue, some yellow and a small amount black. Make triangular shapes from the blue and yellow icing and place these onto the pink icing at an angle to form hats. Stick coloured edible balls into the icing to decorate the hats. Make thin sausages from the black icing and press these across the cupcakes, then make tiny eye patches from black icing. Stick on a tiny sweet for each eye and pipe on red mouths with the gel icing. Keep for up to 2 days in an airtight container.

Ingredients
MAKES 14–16

125 g/4 oz self-raising flour
125 g/4 oz caster sugar
125 g/4 oz soft margarine
2 medium eggs, beaten
1 tsp vanilla extract

To decorate:
125 g/4 oz buttercream (see page 18)
450 g/1 lb ready-to-roll sugarpaste
icing sugar, for dusting
pink, yellow, blue and black paste food colourings
edible coloured and metallic balls and small sweets
small tube red gel icing

Football Cupcakes

1 Preheat the oven to 180°C/350°F/Gas Mark 4. Line two 12-hole bun trays with 12–14 paper fairy-cake cases or silicone moulds, depending on the depth of the holes.

2 Sift the flour into a bowl and stir together with the caster sugar. Add the margarine, eggs and vanilla extract and beat together for about 2 minutes until smooth.

3 Spoon into the cases and bake for 15–20 minutes until golden and firm to the touch. Turn out on a wire rack. When cool, trim the tops flat if they have peaked slightly.

4 To decorate, lightly coat the top of each cupcake with a layer of apricot glaze. Roll out the the almond paste on a surface dusted with icing sugar and cut out circles 6 cm/2½ inches wide and place these on the apricot glaze to cover the top of each cupcake.

5 Colour a quarter of the sugarpaste black and then roll out all the sugarpaste on a surface dusted with icing sugar. Using a small icing nozzle as a round guide, stamp out small white and black discs. Cut six straight edges away from the circles to form hexagons. Dampen the back of each hexagon with a little water, then stick the black discs between white ones, carefully matching up all the edges so they fit together. Keep for up to 3 days in an airtight container.

Ingredients
MAKES 12–14

125 g/4 oz self-raising flour
125 g/4 oz caster sugar
125 g/4 oz soft margarine
2 medium eggs, beaten
1 tsp vanilla extract

To decorate:
½ batch apricot glaze (*see* page 19)
½ batch almond paste (*see* page 19)
icing sugar, for dusting
600 g/1 lb 4 oz ready-to-roll
   sugarpaste
black paste food colouring

4

5

5

Birthday Numbers Cupcakes

1 Preheat the oven to 180°C/350°F/Gas Mark 4. Line one or two 12-hole bun trays with 12–14 paper fairy-cake cases or silicone moulds, depending on the depth of the holes.

2 Sift the flour into a bowl and stir together with the caster sugar. Add the margarine, eggs and vanilla extract and beat together for about 2 minutes until smooth.

3 Spoon into the cases and bake for 15–20 minutes until golden and firm to the touch. Turn out on a wire rack. When cool, trim the tops flat if they have peaked slightly.

4 To decorate, colour batches of sugarpaste in bright colours. Dust a clean surface lightly with icing sugar. Thinly roll each colour of sugarpaste and cut out numbers using a set of cutters or by hand. Leave these for 2 hours to dry and harden.

5 Using a palette knife, spread the buttercream thickly onto the top of each cupcake. Place a small candle into each cupcake and stand the number up against this. Serve within 8 hours, as the numbers may start to soften.

Ingredients
MAKES 12–14

125 g/4 oz self-raising flour
125 g/4 oz caster sugar
125 g/4 oz soft margarine
2 medium eggs, beaten
1 tsp vanilla extract

To decorate:
225 g/8 oz ready-to-roll sugarpaste
paste food colourings
icing sugar, for dusting
1 batch buttercream (see page 18)
small candles

4

5

5

Colourful Letters

1 Preheat the oven to 180°C/350°F/Gas Mark 4. Line two 12-hole bun trays with 12–14 paper fairy-cake cases or silicone moulds, depending on the depth of the holes.

2 Sift the flour into a bowl and stir together with the caster sugar. Add the margarine, eggs and vanilla extract and beat together for about 2 minutes until smooth.

3 Spoon into the cases and bake for 15–20 minutes until golden and firm to the touch. Turn out on a wire rack. When cool, trim the tops flat if they have peaked slightly.

4 To decorate, colour batches of sugarpaste in bright colours. Dust a clean surface lightly with icing sugar. Roll each colour out thinly and cut out letters using a set of cutters or by hand.

5 Blend the icing sugar with 1 tsp water to make a glacé icing of coating consistency. Spread over the top of each cupcake and place a bright letter in the centre of each one. Decorate round the edges with coloured sweets and leave the cupcakes to dry for 30 minutes. Keep for up to 3 days in an airtight container.

Ingredients

MAKES 12–14

125 g/4 oz self-raising flour
125 g/4 oz caster sugar
125 g/4 oz soft margarine
2 medium eggs, beaten
1 tsp vanilla extract

To decorate:

225 g/8 oz ready-to-roll sugarpaste
paste food colourings
350 g/12 oz icing sugar, sifted, plus
    extra for dusting
small coloured sweets

Fast Cars Cupcakes

1 Preheat the oven to 180°C/350°F/Gas Mark 4. Line two 12-hole bun trays with 12–14 paper fairy-cake cases or silicone moulds, depending on the depth of the holes.

2 Sift the flour and cocoa powder into a bowl and stir together with the caster sugar. Add the margarine, eggs and vanilla extract and beat together for about 2 minutes until smooth.

3 Spoon into the cases and bake for 15–20 minutes until golden and firm to the touch. Turn out on a wire rack. When cool, trim the tops flat if they have peaked slightly.

4 To decorate, colour half the sugarpaste blue and half red. Dust a clean surface lightly with icing sugar. Roll each colour out thinly and cut out little car shapes. Leave these for 2 hours to dry and harden.

5 Blend the fondant icing sugar with enough water to make an icing to a coating consistency. Spread over the top of each cupcake and, while still wet, place a car shape in the centre of each one. Mix the royal icing sugar with enough water to make a piping icing. Place this in a small paper icing bag with the end snipped away. Pipe wheels and windows on the cars and leave the cupcakes to dry for 30 minutes. Keep for up to 3 days in an airtight container.

Ingredients

MAKES 12–14

125 g/4 oz self-raising flour
1 tbsp cocoa powder
125 g/4 oz caster sugar
125 g/4 oz soft margarine
2 medium eggs, beaten
1 tsp vanilla extract

To decorate:
225 g/8 oz ready-to-roll sugarpaste
icing sugar, for dusting
red and blue paste food colourings
350 g/12 oz fondant icing
   sugar, sifted
6 tbsp royal icing sugar

3

4

4

Goth Cupcakes

1 Preheat the oven to 180°C/350°F/Gas Mark 4. Line two 12-hole bun trays with 12–14 paper fairy-cake cases or silicone moulds, depending on the depth of the holes.

2 Sift the flour into a bowl and stir together with the caster sugar. Add the margarine, eggs and vanilla extract and beat together for about 2 minutes until smooth.

3 Spoon into the cases and bake for 15–20 minutes until golden and firm to the touch. Turn out on a wire rack. When cool, trim the tops flat if they have peaked slightly.

4 To decorate, blend the fondant icing sugar with enough water to make a coating consistency. Colour half the icing black and half green. Spread over the top of each cupcake and place the silver balls round the outer edges. Decorate with metallic cake shapes and dry for 30 minutes. Keep for up to 2 days in a cool place in an airtight container.

Ingredients
MAKES 12–14

125 g/4 oz self-raising flour
125 g/4 oz caster sugar
125 g/4 oz soft margarine
2 medium eggs, beaten
1 tsp vanilla extract

To decorate:
350 g/12 oz fondant icing
    sugar, sifted
black and green paste
    food colourings
edible silver balls and decorations

Jellybean Cupcakes

1 Preheat the oven to 180°C/350°F/Gas Mark 4. Line two 12-hole bun trays with 12–14 paper fairy-cake cases or silicone moulds, depending on the depth of the holes.

2 Sift the flour into a bowl and stir together with the caster sugar. Add the margarine, eggs and vanilla extract and beat together for about 2 minutes until smooth.

3 Spoon into the cases and bake for 15–20 minutes until golden and firm to the touch. Turn out to cool on a wire rack.

4 When completely cold, swirl buttercream icing all over the tops of the cupcakes and decorate by pressing on coloured jellybeans. Keep for up to 3 days in a cool place in an airtight container.

Ingredients
MAKES 12–14

125 g/4 oz self-raising flour
125 g/4 oz caster sugar
125 g/4 oz soft margarine
2 medium eggs, beaten
1 tsp vanilla extract

To decorate:
1 batch buttercream (see page 18)
colourful jellybeans or candied
    jelly shapes

Pink Flower Cupcakes

1 Preheat the oven to 180°C/350°F/Gas Mark 4 and line a 12-hole muffin tray with deep paper cases.

2 Place the butter, sugar, eggs and vanilla extract in a bowl, then sift in the flour and baking powder. Beat together for about 2 minutes with an electric hand mixer until pale and fluffy. Spoon into the paper cases and bake for 20–25 minutes until firm and golden. Cool on a wire rack.

3 To decorate the cupcakes, first line a 12-hole egg box with foil. Colour 175 g/6 oz of the sugarpaste pink. Roll it out thinly and cut out 12 flower shapes. Use a cocktail stick to mark ridges on the petals and mould the icing in your hand to form flower shapes, then leave in the foil-lined egg boxes for 2 hours.

4 When the flowers are nearly hardened, roll out the remaining white sugarpaste thinly on a surface dusted with icing sugar and cut out circles 6 cm/2½ inches wide. Spread half the cream cheese frosting thinly over each cake and top with a sugarpaste disc. Top each cupcake with a flower, pressing it gently to fix, and pipe a little frosting into the centre of each flower. Keep in a sealed container in a cool place for up to 2 days.

Ingredients
MAKES 12

150 g/5 oz butter, softened
150 g/5 oz caster sugar
3 medium eggs, beaten
1 tsp vanilla extract
150 g/5 oz self-raising flour
½ tsp baking powder

To decorate:

pink paste food colouring
650 g/1 lb 7 oz ready-to-roll
   sugarpaste
icing sugar, for dusting
½ batch cream cheese frosting
   (see page 18)

Prize Rosette Cupcakes

1 Preheat the oven to 180°C/350°F/Gas Mark 4. Line a 12-hole bun tray with paper cases or silicone moulds.

2 Sift the flour into a bowl and stir together with the caster sugar. Add the margarine, eggs and vanilla extract and beat together for about 2 minutes until smooth.

3 Spoon the mixture into the cases and bake for 15–20 minutes until golden and firm to the touch. Turn out on a wire rack. When cool, trim the tops flat if they have formed peaks.

4 To decorate, spread buttercream over the cupcakes and set aside. Break the sugarpaste into three batches and colour each a different colour. Roll out the sugarpaste on a surface lightly dusted with icing sugar and stamp out a fluted circle 6 cm/2½ inches wide with a pastry cutter. Out of the centre of this circle, cut away a small plain disc 3 cm/1 inch wide and reserve. Take a cocktail stick and roll this back and forth in the sugarpaste icing until it begins to frill up. Take the frilled circle and place in the buttercream, fluting up the edges. Make another, smaller, fluted circle in a contrasting colour and place this inside the first layer. Stamp out a plain circle and place this in the centre (or used reserved circles). Write prizes, such as '1st', '2nd' and '3rd', in gel icing in the centres. Keep for up to 3 days in a cool place in an airtight container.

Ingredients
MAKES 12

125 g/4 oz self-raising flour
125 g/4 oz caster sugar
125 g/4 oz soft margarine
2 medium eggs, beaten
1 tsp vanilla extract

To decorate:
125 g/4 oz buttercream (see page 18)
600 g/1 lb 4 oz ready-to-roll sugarpaste
icing sugar, for dusting
red, yellow and blue paste food colourings
gel writing icing tubes

Pink Candle Cupcakes

1 Preheat the oven to 180°C/350°F/Gas Mark 4. Line a 12-hole muffin tray with deep paper cases.

2 Press the raspberries through the sieve to make a purée. Cream the butter and sugar in a bowl, then sift in the flour. In another bowl, beat the eggs with the vanilla extract, then add to the butter and sugar mixture. Beat until smooth, then fold in the purée. Spoon into the cases, filling them three-quarters full.

3 Bake for about 18 minutes until firm to the touch in the centre. Turn out to cool on a wire rack.

4 Colour the frosting pink with a few dots of food colouring. Place in a piping bag fitted with a star nozzle and pipe large swirls on top of each cupcake. Top each cupcake with a tiny candle. Keep for up to 3 days in an airtight container in a cool place.

Ingredients
MAKES 12

75 g/3 oz fresh raspberries
150 g/5 oz butter, softened
150 g/5 oz caster sugar
175 g/6 oz self-raising flour
3 medium eggs
1 tsp vanilla extract

To decorate:
1 batch cream cheese frosting
   (see page 18)
pink liquid food colouring
small pink candles

Blue Bow Cupcakes

1 Preheat the oven to 180°C/350°F/Gas Mark 4. Line a 12-hole muffin tray with deep paper cases.

2 Place the butter and sugar in a bowl, then sift in the flour. In another bowl, beat the eggs with the vanilla extract, then add to the bowl. Beat until smooth, then spoon into the cases, filling them three-quarters full.

3 Bake for about 18 minutes until firm to the touch in the centre. Turn out to cool on a wire rack.

4 To decorate the cupcakes, colour the frosting with a few dots of blue food colouring. Place in a piping bag fitted with a star nozzle and pipe large swirls on top of each cupcake. Make tiny bows from the narrow ribbon and slide each one onto a cocktail stick. Top each cupcake with a tiny bow, being careful to keep the ribbon out of the icing. Keep for up to 2 days in an airtight container in a cool place. Remember to remove the cocktail sticks and bows before eating the cupcakes.

Ingredients
MAKES 12

150 g/5 oz butter, softened
150 g/5 oz caster sugar
175 g/6 oz self-raising flour
3 medium eggs
1 tsp vanilla extract

To decorate:
1 batch cream cheese frosting
   (see page 18)
blue paste food colouring
narrow blue ribbon
cocktail sticks

2

4

4

Starry Cupcakes

1 Preheat the oven to 180˚C/350˚F/Gas Mark 4. Line a 12-hole muffin tray with deep paper cases.

2 Place the butter and sugar in a bowl, then sift in the flour. In another bowl, beat the eggs with the vanilla extract, then add to the flour mixture. Beat until smooth, then spoon into the cases, filling them three-quarters full.

3 Bake for about 18 minutes until firm to the touch in the centre. Turn out to cool on a wire rack.

4 To decorate the cupcakes, dust a clean flat surface with icing sugar. Colour the sugarpaste in batches of bright colours, such as blue, yellow and orange. Roll each out thinly and cut out stars. Leave to dry out for 2 hours until firm. Place the frosting in a piping bag fitted with a star nozzle and pipe large swirls on top of each cupcake. Decorate each cupcake with stars, edible silver balls, if using, and small candles. Keep for up to 2 days in an airtight container in a cool place.

Ingredients
MAKES 12

125 g/4 oz butter, softened
125 g/4 oz caster sugar
125 g/4 oz self-raising flour
2 medium eggs
1 tsp vanilla extract

To decorate:
icing sugar, for dusting
225 g/8 oz ready-to-roll sugarpaste
dust or paste food colourings
1 batch cream cheese frosting (*see* page 18)
edible silver ball decorations (optional)
small candles

3

4

2

Polka Dot Cupcakes

1 Preheat the oven to 180°C/350°F/Gas Mark 4. Line a 12-hole muffin tray with paper cases.

2 Place the butter and sugar in a bowl, then sift in the flour. In another bowl, beat the eggs with the vanilla extract and milk, then add to the flour mixture and beat until smooth. Spoon into the cases, filling them three-quarters full.

3 Bake for about 18 minutes until firm to the touch in the centre. Turn out to cool on a wire rack.

4 To decorate the cupcakes, swirl the top of each cupcake with a little cream cheese frosting using a small palette knife. Divide the sugarpaste into batches and colour each one separately with paste food colouring. Dust a clean flat surface with icing sugar. Roll out the coloured icing and stamp out small circles with the flat end of an icing nozzle. Press the dots onto the frosting. Keep for up to 3 days in a cool place in an airtight container.

Ingredients
MAKES 12

150 g/5 oz butter, softened
150 g/5 oz caster sugar
175 g/6 oz self-raising flour
3 medium eggs
1 tsp vanilla extract
2 tbsp milk

To decorate:

1 batch cream cheese frosting
  (see page 18)
125 g/4 oz ready-to-roll sugarpaste
paste food colourings

New Home Cupcakes

1 Preheat the oven to 180°C/350°F/Gas Mark 4. Line two 12-hole bun trays with 14 paper fairy-cake cases or silicone moulds.

2 Sift the flour into a bowl and stir together with the caster sugar. Add the margarine, eggs and vanilla extract and beat together for about 2 minutes until smooth.

3 Spoon into the cases and bake for 15–20 minutes until golden and firm to the touch. Turn out on a wire rack. When cool, trim the tops flat if they have peaked slightly and lightly coat the top of each cupcake with a little buttercream.

4 To decorate, dust a clean flat surface with icing sugar. Colour half the sugarpaste a pale lemon yellow and roll it out thinly. Cut out circles 6 cm/2½ inches wide and place these over the buttercream and press to smooth down. Colour half the remaining icing brown and the other half red. Roll out thinly on a dusted surface. Cut out small squares in the brown icing and then measure across and cut out a triangular roof shape in red icing. Press the shapes onto the cupcake and pipe on doors, windows and roof tiles in white piping icing. Keep for up to 3 days in an airtight container.

Ingredients

MAKES 14

125 g/4 oz self-raising flour
125 g/4 oz caster sugar
125 g/4 oz soft margarine
2 medium eggs, beaten
1 tsp vanilla extract

To decorate:

125 g/4 oz buttercream
   (see page 18)
icing sugar, for dusting
450 g/1 lb ready-to-roll sugarpaste
red, brown and yellow paste
   food colourings
gel writing icing tubes

3

4

4

Valentine Heart Cupcakes

1 Preheat the oven to 180°C/350°F/Gas Mark 4 and line a 12-hole muffin tray with deep paper cases.

2 Place the butter, sugar, eggs, vanilla extract and milk in a bowl, then sift in the flour and baking powder. Beat together for about 2 minutes with an electric hand mixer until pale and fluffy. Spoon into the paper cases and bake for 20–25 minutes until firm and golden. Cool on a wire rack.

3 To decorate, colour one third of the sugarpaste pink and one third red, leaving the rest white. Wrap a chopping board in clingilm. Dust a clean flat surface with icing sugar. Roll out the sugarpaste thinly and cut out pink, red and white heart shapes, then leave to dry flat and harden for 2 hours (on the clingfilm-coverd chopping board).

4 Colour the cream cheese frosting pale pink and place in a piping bag fitted with a star nozzle. Pipe a swirl on top of each cupcake and decorate with the hearts. Keep in a cool place for up to 2 days.

Ingredients
MAKES 12

150 g/5 oz butter, softened
150 g/5 oz caster sugar
3 medium eggs, beaten
1 tsp vanilla extract
2 tbsp milk
150 g/5 oz self-raising flour
$^1/_2$ tsp baking powder

To decorate:
pink and red paste food colouring
225 g/8 oz ready-to-roll sugarpaste
icing sugar, for dusting
1 batch cream cheese frosting
  (see page 18)

Ruffled Cupcakes

1 Preheat the oven to 180˚C/350˚F/Gas Mark 4. Line a 12-hole bun tray with paper cases or silicone moulds.

2 Sift the flour into a bowl and stir together with the caster sugar. Add the margarine and eggs and beat together with the lemon juice and milk for about 2 minutes until smooth.

3 Spoon into the cases and bake for 15–20 minutes until golden and firm to the touch. Turn out on a wire rack. When cool, trim the tops flat if they have formed peaks. Spread buttercream over the flat surfaces.

4 To decorate the cupcakes, dust a clean flat surface with icing sugar. Roll out the sugarpaste and stamp out a fluted circle 6 cm/2½ inches wide. Cut a small plain 3 cm/1 inch wide circle out of the centre and discard. Take a cocktail stick and roll this back and forth in the sugarpaste circle until it begins to frill up. Take the frilled circle and place on the buttercream, fluting up the edges. Make another fluted circle and cut a break in the ring, then coil this round inside the first layer. Roll a pea-sized ball and place this in the centre. Serve dusted with icing sugar. Keep for up to 3 days in a cool place in an airtight container.

Ingredients
MAKES 12

125 g/4 oz self-raising flour
125 g/4 oz caster sugar
125 g/4 oz soft margarine
2 medium eggs, beaten
1 tsp lemon juice
1 tbsp milk

To decorate:
125 g/4 oz buttercream
  (see page 18)
icing sugar, to dust
450 g/1 lb ready-to-roll sugarpaste

Mini Valentine Heart Cupcakes

1 Preheat the oven to 180°C/350°F/Gas Mark 4 and line a 24-hole mini-muffin tray with mini paper cases.

2 Place the margarine, sugar, eggs, vanilla extract and milk in a bowl, then sift in the flour. Beat together for about 2 minutes with an electric hand mixer until pale and fluffy.

3 Spoon into the paper cases and bake for 14–18 minutes until firm and golden. Cool on a wire rack.

4 To decorate, dust a clean flat surface with icing sugar. Colour one third of the sugarpaste pink and one third red. Leave the rest white. Roll out the sugarpaste thinly and cut out pink, red and white heart shapes. Press onto a cocktail stick and then secure with a little royal icing. Leave to dry flat and harden for 2 hours on greaseproof paper.

5 Colour the cream cheese frosting pale pink and place in a piping bag fitted with a star nozzle. Pipe a swirl on top of each cupcake and decorate each one with a heart. Keep in a cool place for up to 2 days. Remember to remove the cocktail sticks before eating the cupcakes.

Ingredients
MAKES 24

125 g/4 oz soft margarine
125 g/4 oz caster sugar
2 medium eggs, beaten
1 tsp vanilla extract
1 tbsp milk
125 g/4 oz self-raising flour

To decorate:

icing sugar, for dusting
pink and red paste food colouring
225 g/8 oz ready-to-roll sugarpaste
50 g/2 oz ready-made royal icing
1 batch cream cheese frosting
    (see page 18)

1

3

4

Mother's Day Rose Cupcakes

1 Preheat the oven to 190°C/375°F/Gas Mark 5. Line a 12-hole bun tray with paper cases.

2 Place all the cupcake ingredients in a large bowl and beat with an electric mixer for about 2 minutes until smooth. Fill the paper cases halfway up with the mixture. Bake for about 15 minutes until firm, risen and golden. Remove to a wire rack to cool.

3 To decorate the cupcakes, first line an egg box with foil and set aside. Colour the sugarpaste icing with pink paste food colouring. Make a small cone shape, then roll a pea-sized piece of sugarpaste into a ball. Flatten out the ball into a petal shape and wrap this round the cone shape. Continue adding more petals to make a rose, then trim the thick base, place in the egg box and leave to dry out for 2 hours.

4 Blend the fondant icing sugar with a little water to make a thick icing of spreading consistency, then colour this pale pink. Smooth over the top of each cupcake and decorate with the roses immediately. Leave to set for 1 hour. Keep for 1 day in an airtight container.

Ingredients
MAKES 12

125 g/4 oz caster sugar
125 g/4 oz soft tub margarine
2 medium eggs
125 g/4 oz self-raising flour
1 tsp baking powder
1 tsp rosewater

To decorate:
50 g/2 oz ready-to-roll sugarpaste
pink paste food colouring
350 g/12 oz fondant icing sugar

3

3

3

Father's Day Cupcakes

1 Preheat the oven to 180˚C/350˚F/Gas Mark 4. Line two 12-hole bun trays with 14 paper fairy-cake cases or silicone moulds.

2 Sift the flour into a bowl and stir together with the caster sugar. Add the margarine, eggs and vanilla extract and beat together for about 2 minutes until smooth.

3 Spoon into the cases and bake for 15–20 minutes until golden and firm to the touch. Turn out on a wire rack. When cool, trim the tops flat if they have peaked slightly.

4 To decorate, colour half the buttercream yellow and the other half orange and swirl over the top of each cupcake. Dust a clean flat surface with icing sugar. Colour the sugarpaste light blue and roll out thinly. Stamp out large stars 4 cm/1½ inches wide and place these on the buttercream.

5 Make up the royal icing mix and place in a paper piping bag with the end snipped away. Pipe 'Dad' or names on the stars. Decorate with the edible silver balls. Keep for up to 3 days in an airtight container.

Ingredients

MAKES 14

125 g/4 oz self-raising flour
125 g/4 oz caster sugar
125 g/4 oz soft margarine
2 medium eggs, beaten
1 tsp vanilla extract

To decorate:

1 batch buttercream (see page 18)
blue, yellow and orange paste
    food colouring
icing sugar, for dusting
225 g/8 oz ready-to-roll sugarpaste
50 g/2 oz royal icing sugar
edible silver balls

4

4

4

Pink Baby Bow Cupcakes

1 Preheat the oven to 180°C/350°F/Gas Mark 4. Line a 12-hole muffin tray with deep paper cases or silicone moulds.

2 Sift the flour into a bowl and stir together with the caster sugar. Add the margarine, eggs and vanilla extract and beat together with a little pink paste food colouring to give a delicate pink. Beat for about 2 minutes until smooth. Spoon into the cases and bake for 20 minutes, or until golden and firm to the touch. Turn out on a wire rack. When cool, trim the tops flat if they have peaked slightly.

3 To decorate, colour the buttercream pale pink, then colour the sugarpaste pink. Dust a clean flat surface with icing sugar. Roll out the sugarpaste thinly and cut out long narrow strips 1½ cm/½ inch wide. Roll small squares of nonstick baking parchment into narrow tubes and fold the pink icing over these to form loops. Make 24 loops, two for each cupcake, and leave to dry out and firm up for 2 hours. Cut strips to form the ribbon ends of each bow and keep aside on nonstick baking parchment.

4 To finish off the cupcakes, spread the top of each one with pink buttercream, carefully remove the loops from the paper and position the bows in the icing. Place the ribbon pieces onto the cupcakes to finish. Keep for up to 3 days in a cool place in an airtight container.

Ingredients
MAKES 12

125 g/4 oz self-raising flour
125 g/4 oz caster sugar
125 g/4 oz soft margarine
2 medium eggs, beaten
1 tsp vanilla extract
pink paste food colouring

To decorate:
1 batch buttercream (*see* page 18)
pink paste food colouring
icing sugar, for dusting
225 g/8 oz ready-to-roll sugarpaste

2

3

3

Winter Wedding Cupcakes

1 Preheat the oven to 180°C/350°F/Gas Mark 4. Line one or two 12-hole muffin trays with 12–14 deep paper cases, depending on the depth of the holes.

2 Beat the butter and sugar together until light and fluffy, then beat in the eggs a little at a time, adding 1 tsp flour with each addition. Sift in the remaining flour and the spice, add the orange zest and juice, treacle and dried fruit to the bowl and fold together until the mixture is blended. Spoon into the tins and bake for 30 minutes until firm in the centre and a skewer comes out clean. Leave to cool in the trays for 15 minutes, then turn out onto a wire rack. Store undecorated in an airtight container for up to 3 weeks, or freeze until needed.

3 To decorate the cupcakes, trim the top of each cake level, then brush with apricot glaze. Roll out the almond paste and cut out eight discs 6 cm/2½ inches wide. Place these over the glaze and press level. Leave to dry for 24 hours if possible.

4 Dust a clean flat surface with icing sugar. Roll out the sugarpaste and cut out holly leaf and ivy shapes. Leave to dry for 2 hours on nonstick baking parchment or clingfilm. Swirl the royal icing over the top of each cupcake. Press in the holly and ivy shapes and leave to set for 2 hours. Keep in an airtight container for up to up to 3 days, and serve in fancy paper wrappers, if liked.

Ingredients

MAKES 12–14

125 g/4 oz butter
125 g/4 oz soft dark
   muscovado sugar
2 medium eggs, beaten
225 g/8 oz self-raising flour
1 tsp ground mixed spice
finely grated zest and 1 tbsp juice
   from 1 orange
1 tbsp black treacle
350 g/12 oz mixed dried fruit

To decorate:

3 tbsp sieved apricot glaze
   (see page 19)
450 g/1 lb almond paste
   (see page 19)
icing sugar, for dusting
225 g/8 oz ready-to-roll sugarpaste
225 g/8 oz royal icing
fancy paper wrappers (optional)

Butterfly Wings & Flowers Cupcakes

1 Preheat the oven to 180°C/350°F/Gas Mark 4. Line one or two 12-hole muffin trays with 12–14 deep paper cases, depending on the depth of the holes.

2 Place the butter and sugar in a bowl, then sift in the flour. Add beaten eggs to the bowl with the lemon juice and milk and beat until smooth. Spoon into the cases, filling them three-quarters full.

3 Bake for about 18 minutes until firm to the touch in the centre. Turn out to cool on a wire rack.

4 To decorate, colour the sugarpaste in batches of lilac, blue, pink and yellow. Dust a clean flat surface with icing sugar. Roll out the sugarpaste thinly and mark out daisy shapes (see page 176) and butterfly wings. Leave these to dry for 30 minutes until firm enough to handle.

5 Place the frosting in a piping bag fitted with a star nozzle and pipe swirls onto each cupcake. Press the wings and flowers onto the frosting and pipe on decorations with small gel writing icing tubes. Keep in an airtight container in a cool place for 3 days.

Ingredients
MAKES 12–14

150 g/5 oz butter, softened
150 g/5 oz caster sugar
175 g/6 oz self-raising flour
3 medium eggs, beaten
1 tsp lemon juice
2 tbsp milk

To decorate:
350 g/12 oz ready-to-roll sugarpaste
paste food colourings
icing sugar, for dusting
1 batch cream cheese frosting
   (see page 18)
gel writing icing tubes

Quilted Cupcakes

1. Preheat the oven to 180°C/350°F/Gas Mark 4. Line two 12-hole bun trays with 12–14 foil cases, depending on the depth of the holes.

2. Sift the flour into a bowl and stir together with the caster sugar. Add the margarine and eggs and beat together with the lemon juice for about 2 minutes until smooth.

3. Spoon into the cases and bake for 15–20 minutes until golden and firm to the touch. Turn out on a wire rack. When cool, trim the tops flat if they have peaked slightly.

4. To decorate, lightly coat the top of each cupcake with a little buttercream. Dust a clean flat surface with icing sugar. Roll out the sugarpaste and stamp out circles 6 cm/2½ inches wide. Place these on the buttercream to cover the top of each cupcake.

5. Take a palette knife and press lines into the icing, then mark across in the opposite direction to make small squares. Place an edible gold or silver ball into the corner of each square. Keep for up to 3 days in an airtight container in a cool place.

Ingredients
MAKES 12–14

125 g/4 oz self-raising flour
125 g/4 oz caster sugar
125 g/4 oz soft margarine
2 medium eggs, beaten
1 tsp lemon juice

To decorate:

125 g/4 oz buttercream
   (see page 18)
icing sugar, for dusting
450 g/1 lb ready-to-roll sugarpaste
edible gold or silver balls

4

5

4

Hearts & Flowers Cupcakes

1   Preheat the oven to 180°C/350°F/Gas Mark 4. Line a 12-hole muffin tray with deep paper cases.

2   Place the butter and sugar in a bowl, then sift in the flour. Add the beaten eggs to the bowl with the lemon juice and milk and beat until smooth. Spoon into the cases, filling them three-quarters full.

3   Bake for about 18 minutes until firm to the touch in the centre. Turn out to cool on a wire rack.

4   To decorate, colour the sugarpaste in batches in any colours you like. Dust a clean flat surface with icing sugar. Roll out the sugarpaste thinly and stamp out daisies using a flower stamp, then roll out some more sugarpaste thinly and cut out small heart shapes. Leave these to dry out for 30 minutes until firm enough to handle.

5   Make the cream cheese frosting according to the recipe on page 18, if you haven't already, and place in a piping bag fitted with a star nozzle. Pipe swirls onto each cupcake. Press the flowers and hearts onto the frosting. Keep in an airtight container in a cool place for 3 days.

Ingredients
MAKES 12

150 g/5 oz butter, softened
150 g/5 oz caster sugar
175 g/6 oz self-raising flour
3 medium eggs, beaten
1 tsp lemon juice
1 tbsp milk

To decorate:
350 g/12 oz sugarpaste icing
paste food colourings
icing sugar, for dusting
1 batch cream cheese frosting
   (see page 18)

2   4   5

Silver Wedding Celebration Cupcakes

1 Preheat the oven to 180°C/350°F/Gas Mark 4. Line two 12-hole bun trays with silver foil cases.

2 Place the butter and sugar in a bowl, then sift in the flour and stir in the almonds. Add the beaten eggs to the bowl along with the almond extract and milk and beat until smooth. Spoon into the cases, filling them three-quarters full.

3 Bake for about 18 minutes until firm to the touch in the centre. Turn out onto a wire rack. Once cool, trim the tops of the cupcakes if they have peaked. To decorate, first line an egg box with foil. Roll the sugarpaste into pea-sized balls and mould each one into a petal shape. Mould a cone shape and wrap a petal completely round this. Take another petal and wrap round the first, overlapping. Continue wrapping 4–5 petals round until a rose has formed. Pull the thick base away, flute out the petals and place in the egg box. Repeat until you have 24 roses. Leave them to dry out for 2–4 hours. When they are firm, brush edible silver dust lightly over each rose with a clean paintbrush.

4 Make up the fondant icing sugar with water, according to the packet instructions, to a thick icing of a spreading consistency. Spread over the top of each cupcake. Work quickly, as this icing will set. Press a rose into the icing and place a thin silver bow on each cupcake. Leave to set for 30 minutes. Keep in a cool place for 2 days. Remove the bows before eating.

Ingredients

MAKES 24

150 g/5 oz butter, softened
150 g/5 oz caster sugar
150 g/5 oz self-raising flour
25 g/1 oz ground almonds
3 medium eggs, beaten
1 tsp almond extract
2 tbsp milk

To decorate:

350 g/12 oz sugarpaste icing
edible silver dusting powder
450 g/1 lb fondant icing sugar
24 small silver ribbon bows

3

3

3

Golden Wedding Celebration Cupcakes

1 Preheat the oven to 180°C/350°F/Gas Mark 4. Line two 12-hole bun trays with small gold foil cases.

2 Sift the flour into a bowl and stir together with the caster sugar. Add the margarine and eggs and beat together with the lemon juice for about 2 minutes until smooth.

3 Spoon into the cases and bake for 15–20 minutes until golden and firm to the touch. Turn out on a wire rack. When cool, trim the tops flat if they have peaked slightly.

4 To decorate, lightly coat the top of each cupcake with a little buttercream. Dust a clean flat surface with icing sugar. Roll out two thirds of the sugarpaste and stamp out circles 6 cm/2½ inches wide and place these on the buttercream to cover the top of each cupcake.

5 Colour one eighth of the sugarpaste a deep yellow and mould this into thin sausage shapes. Leave these to dry for about 2 hours until firm. Roll out the remaining white sugarpaste and mark out small squares 4 x 4 cm/¾ x ¾ inch. Wrap a square round a yellow centre to form a lily and press the ends together. Make up all the lilies and place on the cupcakes. Cut short thin strips of gold paper ribbon and pull along the blade of a pair of scissors to curl and place on the cakes. Keep for up to 3 days in an airtight container in a cool place. Remove the ribbons before eating.

Ingredients
MAKES 24

125 g/4 oz self-raising flour
125 g/4 oz caster sugar
125 g/4 oz soft margarine
2 medium eggs, beaten
1 tsp lemon juice

To decorate:
125 g/4 oz buttercream
   (see page 18)
icing sugar, for dusting
700 g/1½ lb ready-to-roll sugarpaste
yellow paste food colouring
thin gold ribbon, curled

Christening Day Daisy Cupcakes

1 Preheat the oven to 180°C/350°F/Gas Mark 4. Line a 12-hole muffin tray with deep paper cases.

2 Place the butter and sugar in a bowl, then sift in the flour. Add the beaten eggs to the bowl with the lemon juice and milk and beat until smooth. Spoon into the cases, filling them three-quarters full.

3 Bake for about 18 minutes until firm to the touch in the centre. Turn out to cool on a wire rack.

4 To decorate, dust a clean flat surface with icing sugar. Roll out the sugarpaste thinly and stamp out daisy shapes. Leave these to dry out for 30 minutes until firm enough to handle. Pipe a small yellow gel dot into the centre of each one. Colour the frosting pale yellow, then spread onto the cakes using a palette knife. Press the daisies onto the frosting. Keep in an airtight container in a cool place for 3 days.

Ingredients
MAKES 12

150 g/5 oz butter, softened
150 g/5 oz caster sugar
150 g/5 oz self-raising flour
3 medium eggs, beaten
1 tsp lemon juice
2 tbsp milk

To decorate:
icing sugar, for dusting
125 g/4 oz sugarpaste
yellow gel writing icing tube
1 batch cream cheese frosting
   (see page 18)
yellow paste food colouring

Rose Petal Cupcakes

1 Preheat the oven to 180˚C/350˚F/Gas Mark 4. Line a 12-hole bun tray with foil cases.

2 Sift the flour into a bowl and add the butter, sugar, eggs and rosewater. Beat for about 2 minutes until smooth, then spoon into the paper cases.

3 Bake in the centre of the oven for about 14 minutes until well risen and springy in the centre. Transfer to a wire rack to cool. Keep undecorated for up to 2 days in an airtight container.

4 To decorate, first place a large piece of nonstick baking parchment on a flat surface. Beat the egg white until frothy, then brush thinly over the rose petals. Set the petals on the paper. Dust with caster sugar and leave for 3 hours until dry and sparkling.

5 Beat the icing sugar with the glycerine and rosewater and add enough colouring to give a pale pink colour. Spread over the top of each cupcake and add a circle of rose petals, working quickly, as the icing will begin to set. Leave for 30 minutes before serving. Eat on the day of decorating.

Ingredients

MAKES 12

125 g/4 oz self-raising flour
125 g/4 oz butter, softened
125 g/4 oz golden caster sugar
2 medium eggs, beaten
1 tbsp rosewater

To decorate:

1 egg white
about 80 small dry rose petals
caster sugar, for dusting
175 g/6 oz icing sugar
1 tbsp glycerine
2 tbsp rosewater
pink food colouring

Red & White Cut-out Heart Cupcakes

1 Preheat the oven to 180 C/350 F/Gas Mark 4. Line two 12-hole bun trays with paper or foil cases.

2 Sift the flour into a bowl and stir together with the caster sugar. Add the margarine and eggs and beat together with the vanilla extract for about 2 minutes until smooth.

3 Spoon into the cases and bake for 15–20 minutes until golden and firm to the touch. Turn out on a wire rack. When cool, trim the tops flat if they have peaked slightly.

4 To decorate, lightly coat the top of each cupcake with a little buttercream. Colour half the sugarpaste red. Dust a clean flat surface with icing sugar. Roll out the sugarpaste and stamp out circles 6 cm/2¹/₂ inches wide. Cut out heart shapes from the centre of each circle.

5 Carefully take a white outer circle and place it on the buttercream to cover the top of the cupcake. Take a palette knife and carefully position a red heart in the centre of the white icing. Press together and smooth over. Decorate all the cupcakes using alternate red and white backgrounds. Keep for up to 3 days in an airtight container in a cool place.

Ingredients
MAKES 24

125 g/4 oz self-raising flour
125 g/4 oz caster sugar
125 g/4 oz soft margarine
2 medium eggs, beaten
1 tsp vanilla extract

To decorate:
125 g/4 oz buttercream
  (see page 18)
450 g/1 lb ready-to-roll sugarpaste
icing sugar, for dusting
red paste food colouring

3

4

5

Bluebird Cupcakes

1 Preheat the oven to 180°C/350°F/Gas Mark 4. Line a 12-hole muffin tray with 12–14 deep paper cases, depending on the depth of the holes.

2 Place the butter and sugar in a bowl, then sift in the flour. Add the eggs to the bowl with the lemon juice and milk and beat until smooth. Spoon into the cases, filling them three-quarters full.

3 Bake for about 18 minutes until firm to the touch in the centre. Turn out to cool on a wire rack.

4 To decorate the cupcakes, colour the sugarpaste blue. Dust a clean flat surface with icing sugar. Roll out the sugarpaste thinly and cut out bird wings in sets of two and one body per bird, then stamp out some daisy shapes (see page 176). Leave all these to dry out for 30 minutes until firm enough to handle.

5 Swirl the frosting onto each cupcake. Press one bird's body and pair of wings, and some flowers, onto the frosting and pipe on decorations with the white gel writing icing tubes. Keep in an airtight container in a cool place for 3 days.

Ingredients
MAKES 12–14

150 g/5 oz butter, softened
150 g/5 oz caster sugar
150 g/5 oz self-raising flour
3 medium eggs, beaten
1 tsp lemon juice
1 tbsp milk

To decorate:
125 g/4 oz sugarpaste
blue paste food colouring
icing sugar, for dusting
1 batch cream cheese frosting
   (see page 18)
white gel writing icing tube

Seasonal Fun

Whether you are having a Halloween party or are running out of ideas for Christmas gifts, the seasons and their celebrations offer many ideas for little cakes. Have a go at making the attractive decorations for Spring Daffodil Cupcakes, have fun with the glittery and metallic decorations for Sparkly Christmas Cupcakes, or simply savour the evocative flavours and aromas of Gingerbread Cupcakes or Honey Spice Cupcakes. Take some freshly baked cakes to visit family and relish the delighted faces.

Spring Daffodil Cupcakes

1 Preheat the oven to 180°C/350°F/Gas Mark 4. Line two 12-hole bun trays with 14 paper fairy-cake cases or silicone moulds.

2 Sift the flour into a bowl and stir together with the caster sugar. Add the margarine, eggs and vanilla extract and beat together for about 2 minutes until smooth.

3 Spoon into the cases and bake for 15–20 minutes until golden and firm to the touch. Turn out on a wire rack. When cool, trim the tops flat if they have peaked slightly.

4 To decorate the cupcakes, lightly coat the top of each with a little buttercream. Dust a clean flat surface with icing sugar. Colour half the sugarpaste light green and roll out thinly. Stamp out circles 6 cm/2½ inches wide and place these on the buttercream to cover the top of each cupcake.

5 Colour three quarters of the remaining icing yellow and a quarter orange. Roll out the yellow icing on some baking parchment and mark out thin petal shapes. Take 6 petals and pinch each one together. Place these onto the green icing in a circle, then mould a piece of orange icing into a pea-sized ball. Mould this into a cone shape and place in the centre of the flower. Keep for up to 3 days in an airtight container.

Ingredients

MAKES 14

125 g/4 oz self-raising flour
125 g/4 oz caster sugar
125 g/4 oz soft margarine
2 medium eggs, beaten
1 tsp vanilla extract

To decorate:

125 g/4 oz buttercream
  (see page 18)
icing sugar, for dusting
450 g/1 lb ready-to-roll sugarpaste
green, yellow and orange paste
  food colouring

Easter Nest Cupcakes

1 Preheat the oven to 180˚C/350˚F/Gas Mark 4. Line a 12-hole bun tray with paper cases.

2 Place the margarine and the sugar in a large bowl, then sift in the flour and cocoa powder. In another bowl, beat the eggs with the syrup, then add to the first bowl. Whisk together with an electric beater for 2 minutes, or by hand with a wooden spoon, until smooth.

3 Divide the mixture between the cases, filling them three-quarters full. Bake for about 15 minutes until they are springy to the touch in the centre. Turn out to cool on a wire rack.

4 To decorate, swirl the buttercream over the top of each cupcake. Break up the shredded wheat finely. Melt the chocolate with the butter, then stir in the shredded wheat and let cool slightly. Line a plate with clingfilm. Mould the mixture into tiny nest shapes with your fingers, then place them on the lined plate. Freeze for a few minutes to harden. Set a nest on top of each cupcake and fill with mini eggs. Keep for up to 2 days in a cool place in an airtight container.

Ingredients
MAKES 12

125 g/4 oz soft margarine
125 g/4 oz golden caster sugar
150 g/5 oz self-raising flour
2 tbsp cocoa powder
2 medium eggs
1 tbsp golden syrup

To decorate:
1 batch buttercream (see page 18)
50 g/2 oz shredded wheat cereal
125 g/4 oz milk chocolate, broken
    into pieces
25 g/1 oz unsalted butter
chocolate mini eggs

2

4

4

Harvest Festival Cupcakes

1 Preheat the oven to 180°C/350°F/Gas Mark 4. Lightly oil a deep 12-hole muffin tray or line with deep paper cases.

2 Sift the flour, baking powder, cinnamon and salt into a bowl, along with any bran from the sieve.

3 Add the oil, sugar, eggs, vanilla extract, sultanas and grated carrots. Beat until smooth and then spoon into the muffin tray. Bake for 20–25 minutes until risen and golden. Cool on a wire rack.

4 To decorate, colour the frosting pale green and smooth over the top of each cupcake. Colour the sugarpaste in small batches of orange, red, green and brown and mould into cabbages, carrots, potatoes and tomatoes. Press green sugarpaste through a garlic press to make green carrot leaves. Place the vegetables on top of each cupcake. Keep for up to 3 days in an airtight container in a cool place.

Ingredients
MAKES 12

175 g/6 oz self-raising wholemeal flour
1 tsp baking powder
$\frac{1}{2}$ tsp ground cinnamon
pinch salt
150 ml/$\frac{1}{4}$ pint sunflower oil
150 g/5 oz soft light brown sugar
3 medium eggs, beaten
1 tsp vanilla extract
50 g/2 oz sultanas
225 g/8 oz carrots, peeled and finely grated

To decorate:
1 batch cream cheese frosting (*see* page 18)
paste food colourings
225 g/8 oz ready-to-roll sugarpaste

Halloween Cobweb Cupcakes

1. Preheat the oven to 180°C/350°F/Gas Mark 4. Line two 12-hole bun trays with 16–18 paper or foil cases, depending on the depth of the holes.

2. Place the sugar, margarine and eggs in a bowl, then sift in the flour, baking powder and cocoa powder. Beat for 2 minutes, or until smooth.

3. Spoon the mixture into the paper cases and bake for 15–20 minutes until well risen and the tops spring back when lightly pressed. Transfer to a wire rack to cool, then trim the tops of the cupcakes flat if they have any peaks.

4. To decorate the cupcakes, gradually mix the icing sugar with enough warm water to give a coating consistency. Colour a little of the icing black and place in a small paper icing bag. Colour the remaining icing bright orange.

5. Work on one cupcake at a time. Spread orange icing over the top of the cupcake. Snip a small hole from the base of the icing bag, then pipe a black spiral on top of the wet orange icing. Use a wooden toothpick and pull this through the icing to give a cobweb effect. Repeat with all the cupcakes and leave to set for 1 hour. Keep for up to 2 days in an airtight container in a cool place.

Ingredients

MAKES 16–18

175 g/6 oz caster sugar
175 g/6 oz soft margarine
3 medium eggs, beaten
150 g/5 oz self-raising flour
1 tsp baking powder
25 g/1 oz cocoa powder

To decorate:

225 g/8 oz icing sugar, sifted
2 tbsp warm water
orange and black paste
    food colourings

3

5

5

Christmas Rose Cupcakes

1 Preheat the oven to 180°C/350°F/Gas Mark 4. Line two 12-hole bun trays with 18 silver foil cases.

2 Place the butter and sugar in a bowl, then sift in the flour and stir in the almonds. Add the beaten eggs to the bowl with the almond extract and milk and beat until smooth. Spoon into the cases, filling them three-quarters full.

3 Bake for about 18 minutes until firm to the touch in the centre. Turn out onto a wire rack. Once cool, trim the tops of the cupcakes if they have peaked.

4 To decorate the cupcakes, first line an egg box with kitchen foil and set aside. Roll the sugarpaste into pea-sized balls and mould each one into a petal shape. Make 4–5 petals for each cupcake. Place the petals in the egg box to dry out for 2 hours until firm.

5 Mix the fondant icing sugar with water, according to the packet instructions, to a thick icing of a spreading consistency. Spread over the top of each cupcake. Work quickly, as the icing will start to set. Press 4–5 petals into the icing on each cupcake. Colour the royal icing pale lemon and place in a small paper icing bag and snip off the end. Pipe dots in the centre of each flower and leave to set for 30 minutes. Keep in a cool place for up to 2 days.

Ingredients

MAKES 18

150 g/5 oz butter, softened
150 g/5 oz caster sugar
150 g/5 oz self-raising flour
25 g/1 oz ground almonds
3 medium eggs, beaten
1 tsp almond extract
2 tbsp milk

To decorate:

350 g/12 oz sugarpaste
450 g/1 lb fondant icing sugar
125 g/4 oz ready-made royal icing
yellow paste food colouring

4

5

5

Sparkly Snowflake Cupcakes

1 Preheat the oven to 180°C/350°F/Gas Mark 4. Line two 12-hole bun trays with silver foil cases.

2 Place the butter and sugar in a bowl, then sift in the flour and stir in the almonds. Add the beaten eggs to the bowl with the almond extract and milk. Spoon into the cases, filling them three-quarters full.

3 Bake for about 18 minutes until firm to the touch in the centre. Turn out onto a wire rack. Once cool, trim the tops of the cupcakes if they have peaked.

4 To decorate the cupcakes, dust a clean flat surface with icing sugar. Roll the sugarpaste thinly and mark out a snowflake pattern. Cut round the shapes and leave them to dry flat on a sheet of nonstick baking parchment for 2 hours until firm.

5 Make up the royal icing according to the packet instructions to a soft icing that will form peaks. Swirl the icing onto the cupcakes and place a snowflake shape centrally on each cupcake. Decorate with silver balls and leave for 30 minutes to set. Keep for up to 2 days in an airtight container.

Ingredients
MAKES 24

150 g/5 oz butter, softened
150 g/5 oz caster sugar
150 g/5 oz self-raising flour
25 g/1 oz ground almonds
3 medium eggs, beaten
1 tsp almond extract
1 tbsp milk

To decorate:
icing sugar, for dusting
350 g/12 oz sugarpaste
450 g/1 lb royal icing sugar
edible silver balls

Festive Candy Cane Cupcakes

1 Preheat the oven to 180°C/350°F/Gas Mark 4. Line two 12-hole bun trays with 14–18 foil cases, depending on the depth of the holes.

2 Place the butter and sugar in a bowl, then sift in the flour and stir in the almonds. Add the eggs, along with the vanilla extract and milk. Spoon into the cases, filling them three-quarters full.

3 Bake for about 18 minutes until firm to the touch in the centre. Turn out onto a wire rack. Once cool, trim the tops of the cupcakes if they have peaked.

4 To decorate, colour one quarter of the sugarpaste red and one quarter green. Dust a clean flat surface with icing sugar. Roll out the sugarpaste into long, very thin sausages with the palms of your hands. Roll a sausage of red with a sausage of white to form a twist. Cut into short lengths about 5 cm/2½ inches long and bend round to form cane shapes. Do the same with green and white sugarpaste. Leave to dry out flat for 2 hours until firm.

5 Make up the royal icing according to the packet instructions to a soft icing that will form peaks. Smooth the icing onto the cupcakes and place a cane centrally on each cupcake. Place the remaining icing in a small piping bag fitted with a star nozzle and pipe a star border round the outside of each cupcake. Keep for up to 2 days in an airtight container.

Ingredients
MAKES 14–18

150 g/5 oz butter, softened
150 g/5 oz caster sugar
150 g/5 oz self-raising flour
25 g/1 oz ground almonds
3 medium eggs, beaten
1 tsp vanilla extract
2 tbsp milk

To decorate:
225 g/8 oz sugarpaste
red and green paste food colourings
icing sugar, for dusting
450 g/1 lb royal icing sugar

4

4

4

Sparkly Christmas Cupcakes

1 Preheat the oven to 180°C/350°F/Gas Mark 4. Line a 12-hole bun tray with 14–18 foil fairy-cake cases, depending on the size of the holes.

2 Beat the butter and sugar together until light and fluffy, then beat in the eggs a little at a time, adding 1 tsp flour with each addition. Sift in the remaining flour and spice, add the orange zest and juice, treacle and dried fruit to the bowl and fold together until the mixture is blended.

3 Spoon into the cases and bake for about 30 minutes until firm in the centre and a skewer comes out clean. Leave to cool in the trays for 15 minutes, then turn out to cool on a wire rack. Store undecorated in an airtight container for up to 3 weeks, or freeze until needed.

4 To decorate, trim the top of each fairy cake level if necessary, then brush with apricot glaze. Roll out the almond paste and cut out eight circles to fit the cakes. Place a disc on top of each fairy cake and press level. Leave to dry for 24 hours if possible.

5 Swirl the royal icing over the fairy cakes, flicking into peaks with a small palette knife. Decorate with silver balls while the icing is still wet. Leave to dry out for 1 hour. Keep for up to 4 days in an airtight container.

Ingredients
MAKES 14–18

125 g/4 oz butter, softened
125 g/4 oz soft dark
    muscovado sugar
2 medium eggs, beaten
225 g/8 oz self-raising flour
1 tsp ground mixed spice
finely grated zest and 1 tbsp juice
    from 1 orange
1 tbsp black treacle
350 g/12 oz mixed dried fruit

To decorate:
3 tbsp sieved apricot glaze
    (see page 19)
225 g/8 oz almond paste
    (see page 19)
1 batch royal icing (see page 18)
edible silver ball decorations

4

4

5

Gingerbread Cupcakes

1 Preheat the oven to 180˚C/350˚F/Gas Mark 4. Line one or two muffin trays with 14–16 deep paper cases, depending on the depth of the holes.

2 Place the syrup and margarine in a heavy-based pan and melt together gently. Sift the flour and ginger into a bowl, then stir in the sultanas and sugar.

3 Warm the milk and stir in the bicarbonate of soda. Pour the syrup mixture, the milk and beaten egg into the dry ingredients and beat until smooth.

4 Spoon the mixture halfway up each case and bake for 25–30 minutes until risen and firm. Cool in the trays for 10 minutes, then turn out to cool on a wire rack.

5 To decorate the cupcakes, blend the icing sugar with 1 tbsp warm water to make a thin glacé icing. Place in a paper icing bag and snip away the tip. Drizzle over the top of each cupcake in a lacy pattern. Keep in an airtight container for up to 5 days.

Ingredients
MAKES 14–16

8 tbsp golden syrup
125 g/4 oz block margarine
225 g/8 oz plain flour
2 tsp ground ginger
75 g/3 oz sultanas
50 g/2 oz soft dark brown sugar
175 ml/6 fl oz milk
1 tsp bicarbonate of soda
1 medium egg, beaten
125 g/4 oz golden icing sugar,
   to decorate

Honey Spice Cupcakes

1 Preheat the oven to 160°C/325°F/Gas Mark 3. Line one or two muffin trays with 12–14 deep paper cases, depending on the depth of the holes. Dissolve the coffee in the water and leave aside to cool.

2 Sift the flour with the baking powder, bicarbonate of soda and spices. In another bowl, add the honey to the sugar and beat in the eggs until smooth and light, then gradually beat in the oil until blended. Stir this into the flour mixture along with the coffee and walnuts. Beat until smooth.

3 Carefully spoon the mixture into the paper cases. Fill each halfway up. Be careful not to overfill them, as the mixture will rise up. Bake for 25–30 minutes until they are risen, firm and golden. Leave in the trays for 5 minutes, then turn out onto a wire rack to cool.

4 To decorate, blend the icing sugar with 1 tbsp warm water to make a thin glacé icing. Place in a paper icing bag and snip away the tip. Pipe large daisies round the top of each cupcake and leave to set for 30 minutes. Keep in an airtight container for up to 5 days.

Ingredients

MAKES 12–14

1 tsp instant coffee granules
6 tbsp hot water
175 g/6 oz plain flour
1 tsp baking powder
$\frac{1}{2}$ tsp bicarbonate of soda
$\frac{1}{2}$ tsp ground cinnamon
$\frac{1}{2}$ tsp ground ginger
pinch ground cloves
175 g/6 oz honey
125 g/4 oz golden caster sugar
2 medium eggs
5 tbsp vegetable oil
50 g/2 oz walnuts, finely chopped
125 g/4 oz golden icing sugar,
    to decorate

Scandinavian Apple Cupcakes

1 Preheat the oven to 180°C/350°F/Gas Mark 4. Line two 12-hole bun trays with red paper or foil cases.

2 Sift the flour and cinnamon into a bowl and stir together with the caster sugar. Add the margarine and eggs and beat together with the vanilla extract for about 2 minutes until smooth.

3 Spoon into the cases and bake for 15–20 minutes until golden and firm to the touch. Turn out to cool on a wire rack. When cool, trim the tops flat if they have peaked slightly.

4 To decorate, lightly coat the top of each cupcake with a little buttercream. Dust a clean flat surface with icing sugar. Colour one quarter of the sugarpaste red, one quarter green and a few scraps brown, leaving the rest white. Roll out the white sugarpaste and stamp out circles 6 cm/2¹⁄₂ inches wide. Place on top of each cupcake and smooth level. Mould the green and red sugarpaste into round apple shapes and place on top of the white icing. Decorate with small green leaves and brown stalks. Keep for up to 3 days in an airtight container in a cool place.

Ingredients
MAKES 12–14

125 g/4 oz self-raising flour
¹⁄₂ tsp ground cinnamon
125 g/4 oz caster sugar
125 g/4 oz soft margarine
2 medium eggs, beaten
1 tsp vanilla extract

To decorate:

125 g/4 oz buttercream
 (see page 18)
icing sugar, for dusting
600 g/1 lb 5 oz ready-to-roll
 sugarpaste
red, green and brown paste
 food colourings

Chocolate Holly Leaf Muffins

1 Preheat the oven to 190°C/375°F/Gas Mark 5. Line a 12-hole muffin tray with deep paper cases.

2 Place all the cupcake ingredients except the chocolate chips in a large bowl and beat with an electric mixer for about 2 minutes until smooth. Fold in the chocolate chips, then fill the paper cases halfway up with the mixture. Bake for about 15 minutes until firm, risen and golden. Remove to a wire rack to cool.

3 To decorate the cupcakes, paint the underside of each holly leaf with the melted dark chocolate. Leave to dry out on nonstick baking parchment for 1 hour, or in the refrigerator for 30 minutes.

4 Beat the butter until soft, then gradually beat in the icing sugar until light. Add the cream cheese and whisk until fluffy. Divide the mixture in half and beat the cooled melted milk chocolate into one half and the vanilla extract into the other half. Fit a piping bag with a wide star nozzle and spoon chocolate icing on one side of the bag and the vanilla icing on the other. Pipe swirls on top of the cupcakes.

5 Peel the holly leaves away from the set chocolate and decorate the top of each cupcake with a chocolate leaf. Keep for up to 3 days in an airtight container in a cool place.

Ingredients

MAKES 12

125 g/4 oz caster sugar
125 g/4 oz soft tub margarine
2 medium eggs
125 g/4 oz self-raising flour
1/2 tsp baking powder
50 g/2 oz plain or milk
  chocolate chips

To decorate:

12 holly leaves, washed and dried
75 g/3 oz dark chocolate, melted
50 g/2 oz unsalted butter, softened
300 g/11 oz icing sugar, sifted
125 g/4 oz full-fat cream cheese
50 g/2 oz milk chocolate, melted
  and cooled
1 tsp vanilla extract

Hogmanay Party Cupcakes

1 Preheat the oven to 180°C/350°F/Gas Mark 4. Line two 12-hole bun trays with 14 paper fairy-cake cases or silicone moulds.

2 Sift the flour into a bowl and stir together with the caster sugar. Add the margarine and eggs. Beat with the vanilla extract for about 2 minutes until smooth.

3 Spoon into the cases and bake for 15–20 minutes until golden and firm to the touch. Turn out onto a wire rack. When cool, trim the tops flat if they have peaked slightly.

4 To decorate, lightly coat the top of each fairy cake with a little buttercream. Dust a clean flat surface with icing sugar. Colour half the sugarpaste a pale cream shade and roll out thinly. Stamp out circles 6 cm/2½ inches wide and place these on the buttercream to cover the top of each fairy cake.

5 Colour the remaining icing green and lilac. Mould the green icing into stems as pictured or, to be more thistle-like, place a small ball onto each thin stem to form the bulbous part. Mark the bulbous parts with 'spikes', and position on the fairy cakes. Roll out the lilac sugarpaste into a long thin strip about 2.5 cm/1 inch wide. Cut with a knife, or snip with scissors, three-quarters of the way through the paste, then roll up to form a tassel for a thistle top and attach to the top of a stem. Repeat on all the cakes. Keep for up to 3 days in an airtight container.

Ingredients
MAKES 14

125 g/4 oz self-raising flour
125 g/4 oz caster sugar
125 g/4 oz soft margarine
2 medium eggs, beaten
1 tsp vanilla extract

To decorate:
125 g/4 oz buttercream
   (see page 18)
icing sugar, for dusting
450 g/1 lb ready-to-roll sugarpaste
yellow, green and lilac paste
   food colourings

4

4

5

Christmas Tree Cupcakes

1 Preheat the oven to 180°C/350°F/Gas Mark 4. Line two 12-hole bun trays with 14 paper fairy-cake cases or silicone moulds.

2 Sift the flour into a bowl and stir together with the caster sugar. Add the margarine, eggs and vanilla extract and beat together for about 2 minutes until smooth.

3 Spoon into the cases and bake for 15–20 minutes until golden and firm to the touch. Turn out onto a wire rack. When cool, trim the tops flat if they have peaked slightly.

4 To decorate, lightly coat the top of each fairy cake with a little buttercream. Colour one quarter of the sugarpaste green and keep aside. Dust a clean flat surface with icing sugar. Roll the white sugarpaste thinly and stamp out 14 circles 6 cm/2½ inches wide. Set these on the buttercream to cover the top of each fairy cake.

5 Roll out the green sugarpaste thinly and cut into narrow strips 2.5 cm/1 inch wide. Take a toothpick and roll this back and forth to flute up the edges of the sugarpaste. Cut the fluted strips into graduated layers to make triangular tree shapes and press onto the fairy cakes. Decorate with edible silver balls. Keep for up to 3 days in an airtight container.

Ingredients

MAKES 14

125 g/4 oz self-raising flour
125 g/4 oz caster sugar
125 g/4 oz soft margarine
2 medium eggs, beaten
1 tsp vanilla extract

To decorate:

125 g/4 oz buttercream
  (see page 18)
600 g/1 lb 5 oz ready-to-roll
  sugarpaste
green paste food colouring
icing sugar, for dusting
edible silver balls

Christmas Pudding Cupcakes

1 Preheat the oven to 180°C/350°F/Gas Mark 4. Line one or two 12-hole bun trays with 14–18 foil fairy-cake cases, depending on the depth of the holes.

2 Beat the butter and sugar together until light and fluffy, then beat in the eggs a little at a time, adding 1 tsp flour with each addition. Sift in the remaining flour and spice, add the orange zest and juice, treacle and dried fruit to the bowl and fold together until the mixture is blended. Spoon into the cases and bake for about 30 minutes until firm in the centre and a skewer comes out clean. Leave to cool in the trays for 15 minutes, then turn out to cool on a wire rack. Store undecorated in an airtight container for up to 4 weeks, or freeze until needed.

3 To decorate, trim the top of each cake level if they have peaked, then brush with apricot glaze. Roll out the almond paste and cut out circles 6 cm/2½ inches wide. Place a disc on top of each fairy cake and press level. Leave to dry for 24 hours if possible.

4 Dust a clean flat surface with icing sugar. Colour half the sugarpaste brown, roll out thinly and cut out circles 6 cm/2½ inches wide. Place on top of the almond paste and press level. Colour the remaining sugarpaste cream or pale yellow, mould into a fluted disc and press on top to represent custard. Colour scraps of sugarpaste green and red and shape into holly leaves and berries. Keep for up to 1 week in an airtight container.

Ingredients
MAKES 14–18

125 g/4 oz butter, softened
125 g/4 oz soft dark
    muscovado sugar
2 medium eggs, beaten
225 g/8 oz self-raising flour
1 tsp ground mixed spice
finely grated zest and 1 tbsp juice
    from 1 orange
1 tbsp black treacle
350 g/12 oz mixed dried fruit

To decorate:

3 tbsp sieved apricot glaze
    (see page 19)
225 g/8 oz almond paste
    (see page 19)
icing sugar, for dusting
450 g/1 lb ready-to-roll sugarpaste
brown, red, green and yellow paste
    food colourings

Giftwrapped Presents Cupcakes

1 Preheat the oven to 180°C/350°F/Gas Mark 4. Line one or two 12-hole muffin trays with 12–14 deep paper cases, depending on the depth of the holes.

2 Beat the butter and sugar together until light and fluffy, then beat in the eggs a little at a time, adding 1 tsp flour with each addition. Sift in the remaining flour and spice, add the orange zest and juice, treacle and dried fruit to the bowl and fold together until the mixture is blended.

3 Spoon into the cases and bake for about 30 minutes until firm in the centre and a skewer comes out clean. Leave to cool in the trays for 15 minutes, then turn out to cool on a wire rack. Store undecorated in an airtight container for up to 4 weeks, or freeze until needed.

4 To decorate, trim the top of each cupcake level if they have peaked, then brush with apricot glaze. Dust a clean flat surface with icing sugar. Colour the sugarpaste in batches and roll out thinly. Cut out circles 6 cm/2½ inches wide. Place a disc on top of each cupcake and press level. Mould coloured scraps into long thin sausages and roll these out thinly. Place a contrasting colour across each cupcake and arrange into bows and loops. Leave to dry for 24 hours if possible. Keep for up to 4 days in an airtight container.

Ingredients
MAKES 12–14

125 g/4 oz butter, softened
125 g/4 oz soft dark
    muscovado sugar
2 medium eggs, beaten
225 g/8 oz self-raising flour
1 tsp ground mixed spice
finely grated zest and 1 tbsp juice
    from 1 orange
1 tbsp black treacle
350 g/12 oz mixed dried fruit

To decorate:

3 tbsp sieved apricot glaze
    (see page 19)
icing sugar, for dusting
600 g/1 lb 5 oz ready-to-roll
    sugarpaste
red, blue, green and yellow paste
    food colourings

Crystallised Rosemary & Cranberry Cupcakes

1   Preheat the oven to 180°C/350°F/Gas Mark 4. Line a 12-hole bun tray with foil fairy cake cases.

2   Sift the flour into a bowl and add the butter, sugar, eggs and orange zest. Beat for about 2 minutes until smooth, then spoon into the paper cases.

3   Bake in the centre of the oven for about 14 minutes until well risen and springy in the centre. Transfer to a wire rack to cool.

4   To decorate, place a sheet of nonstick baking parchment on a flat surface. Beat the egg white until frothy, then brush thinly over the rosemary and cranberries (or dip them into it) and place them on the nonstick baking parchment. Dust with caster sugar (or dip them into the sugar) and leave to dry out for 2–4 hours until crisp.

5   Brush the top of each fairy cake with a little apricot glaze. Roll out the sugarpaste on a clean flat surface dusted with icing sugar and cut out 12 circles 6 cm/2½ inches wide. Place a disc on top of each and press level. Decorate each one with sparkly rosemary sprigs and cranberries. Keep for up to 3 days in an airtight container in a cool place.

Ingredients

MAKES 12

125 g/4 oz self-raising flour
125 g/4 oz butter, softened
125 g/4 oz golden caster sugar
2 medium eggs, beaten
zest of ½ orange, finely grated

To decorate:

1 egg white
12 small rosemary sprigs
125 g/4 oz fresh red cranberries
caster sugar, for dusting
3 tbsp apricot glaze, sieved
   (see page 19)
350 g/12 oz ready-to-roll sugarpaste

Glittery Outer Space Cupcakes

1 Preheat the oven to 180°C/350°F/Gas Mark 4. Line a mini-muffin tray with 18–20 mini paper cases or silicone moulds, depending on the depth of the holes.

2 Place the margarine and sugar in a bowl, then sift in the flour. In another bowl, beat the eggs with the vanilla extract and milk, then add to the flour mixture. Beat until smooth, then spoon into the cases, filling them halfway up.

3 Bake for about 12–14 minutes until firm to the touch in the centre. Turn out to cool on a wire rack.

4 Place a large piece of nonstick baking parchment on a flat surface. Roll the sugarpaste into pea-sized balls on the paper. Coat the balls with edible coloured or glitter dust. Leave to dry out for 2 hours until firm. Place the frosting in a piping bag fitted with a star nozzle and pipe swirls on top of each cupcake. Top each cupcake with the coloured sugarpaste balls and edible metallic balls. Keep for up to 2 days in an airtight container in a cool place.

Ingredients
MAKES 18–20

125 g/4 oz soft margarine
125 g/4 oz caster sugar
125 g/4 oz self-raising flour
2 medium eggs
1 tsp vanilla extract
1 tbsp milk

To decorate:
125 g/4 oz ready-to-roll sugarpaste
edible coloured or glitter dust
1 batch cream cheese frosting
   (see page 18)
edible metallic coloured balls

White Chocolate Christmas Cupcakes

1 Preheat the oven to 180˚C/350˚F/Gas Mark 4. Line one or two 12-hole bun trays with 12–16 foil cases, depending on the depth of the holes.

2 Place the butter and sugar in a bowl, then sift in the flour. Add the eggs to the bowl with the vanilla extract and milk and beat until smooth. Fold in the grated white chocolate, then spoon into the cases, filling them three-quarters full. Bake for about 18 minutes until firm to the touch in the centre. Turn out to cool on a wire rack.

3 To decorate, melt the white chocolate in a heatproof bowl over a pan of barely simmering water. Use one third of the melted chocolate to paint the underside of the holly leaves and leave to set for 30 minutes in the refrigerator. Spread one third of the chocolate out onto a clean plastic board. When almost set, make into curls by pulling a sharp knife through the chocolate at an angle until the chocolate curls away from the knife. Stir the remaining cooled chocolate into the buttercream and chill for 15 minutes.

4 Swirl each cupcake with buttercream, then press on the white chocolate curls. Peel the holly leaves away from the chocolate and carefully place on top of the cupcakes. Dust with icing sugar before serving. Keep for up to 2 days in the refrigerator.

Ingredients
MAKES 12–16

150 g/5 oz butter, softened
150 g/5 oz caster sugar
150 g/5 oz self-raising flour
3 medium eggs, beaten
1 tsp vanilla extract
1 tbsp milk
75 g/3 oz white chocolate, finely grated

To decorate:

250 g/9 oz white chocolate, chopped
16 holly leaves, cleaned and dried
1 batch buttercream (*see* page 18)
icing sugar, for dusting

2

3

3

Index